EYEWITNESS
PLANT

Blackberries

Red ginseng root

Gerbera flower

Moss on decaying wood

Radish

Peppers

Ornamental dried corn

Opium poppy seed heads

Redshank flowers

Ribwort plantain seed heads

Delphinium flowers

EYEWITNESS
PLANT

In association with
THE NATURAL HISTORY MUSEUM

Written by
DAVID BURNIE

Garden pansies

Garden yarrow
flower head

Aster

Columbine
seed heads

Feverfew
flowers

DK

Ripe fig
cut in half

Common
sorrel

Tufted
vetch

Creeping
buttercup

Common
toadflax

Poppy
seed head

Flower
of blue
echeveria

Lords-and-ladies

Eucalyptus
leaves

Field
scabious

Yarrow
leaf

Ox-eye
daisy

Spear
thistle

DK

Penguin Random House

REVISED EDITION

DK DELHI
Senior Art Editor Vikas Chauhan
Editor Shahid Qureshi
Deputy Manager, Picture Research Virien Chopra
Deputy Managing Editor Sreshtha Bhattacharya
Managing Editor Kingshuk Ghoshal
Managing Art Editor Govind Mittal
DTP Designers Pawan Kumar, Vikram Singh
Jacket Designer Vidushi Chaudhry
Creative Head Malavika Talukder

DK LONDON
Editor Binta Jallow
Art Editor Chrissy Checketts
US Senior Editor Jennette ElNaggar
US Executive Editor Lori Cates Hand
Managing Editor Francesca Baines
Managing Art Editor Philip Letsu
Production Editor Becky Fallowfield
Production Controller Ena Matagic
Publisher Andrew Macintyre
Art Director Mabel Chan

Consultant Dr. Chris Clennett

FIRST EDITION
Project Editor Helen Parker
Senior Editor Sophie Mitchell
Senior Art Editor Julia Harris
Managing Editor Sue Unstead
Managing Art Editor Roger Priddy
Special Photography Jane Burton, Karl Shone,
and Kim Taylor
Editorial Consultants The staff of the Natural History
Museum, London and the Royal Botanic Gardens, Kew

This American Edition, 2025
First American Edition, 1989
Published in the United States by DK Publishing,
a division of Penguin Random House LLC
1745 Broadway, 20th Floor, New York, NY 10019

Published in Great Britain by Dorling Kindersley Limited

A catalog record for this book is available
from the Library of Congress.
ISBN 978-0-5939-6907-6 (Paperback)
ISBN 978-0-5939-6908-3 (ALB)

DK books are available at special discounts when
purchased in bulk for sales promotions, premiums,
fund-raising, or educational use. For details, contact:
DK Publishing Special Markets,
1745 Broadway, 20th Floor, New York, NY 10019
SpecialSales@dk.com

Printed and bound in China

www.dk.com

Contents

Bladder senna

Young peas in pod

What is a **plant?**

Plants are the key to life on Earth. Many living things depend on plants for food and shelter, and plants make their own food, using energy that they collect from sunlight. There are two main kinds of plants—non-flowering and flowering. Flowering plants grow in most habitats, and there are now more than 350,000 species.

Lichen

This was a plant
Forests of giant club mosses, up to 150 ft (45 m) tall, once filled our planet. Over time, their remains turned to coal.

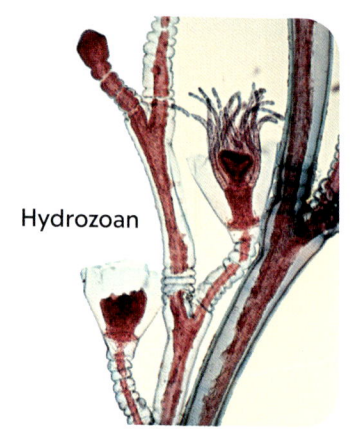

Hydrozoan

This is a plant
A lichen is made up of two organisms: a fungus and an alga, a tiny nonflowering plant. The algal cells supply the fungus with food, which they make using sunlight (pp.14–15). Lichens grow very slowly.

Lichens growing on limestone rock

Horsetail

This is not a plant
A hydrozoan is an organism living in the sea. It is formed by polyps, tiny animals with tentacles that trap food.

Mosses have no roots and cling to damp rocks.

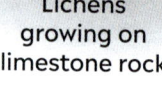
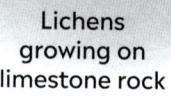

Contemporary cousins
The first ferns and horsetails grew 300 million years ago. There are still many types of ferns, but fewer than 20 horsetail species.

Hart's-tongue fern

Spores

Microscopic view of watermeal

Biggest and smallest
California's giant sequoias can grow 310 ft (95 m) tall. Watermeal, the smallest flowering plant, is only 1/100 in (0.3 mm) across.

Liverworts
These nonflowering plants have spores and grow in damp places.

Ribbon-like plant body, or thallus, divides into branches as it grows.

Mosses
These plants do not have flowers but use spores to reproduce.

Algae mosaic
This microscope image shows many species of diatoms, a single-celled alga with a rigid cell wall made of silica.

Garden pansy, a flowering plant

Flowering plants
All flowering plants have true flowers. Their seeds develop inside an ovary (p.17), which later becomes a fruit (pp.26–27).

Blanketweed

Green blanket
Long chains of aquatic algae cells create slime.

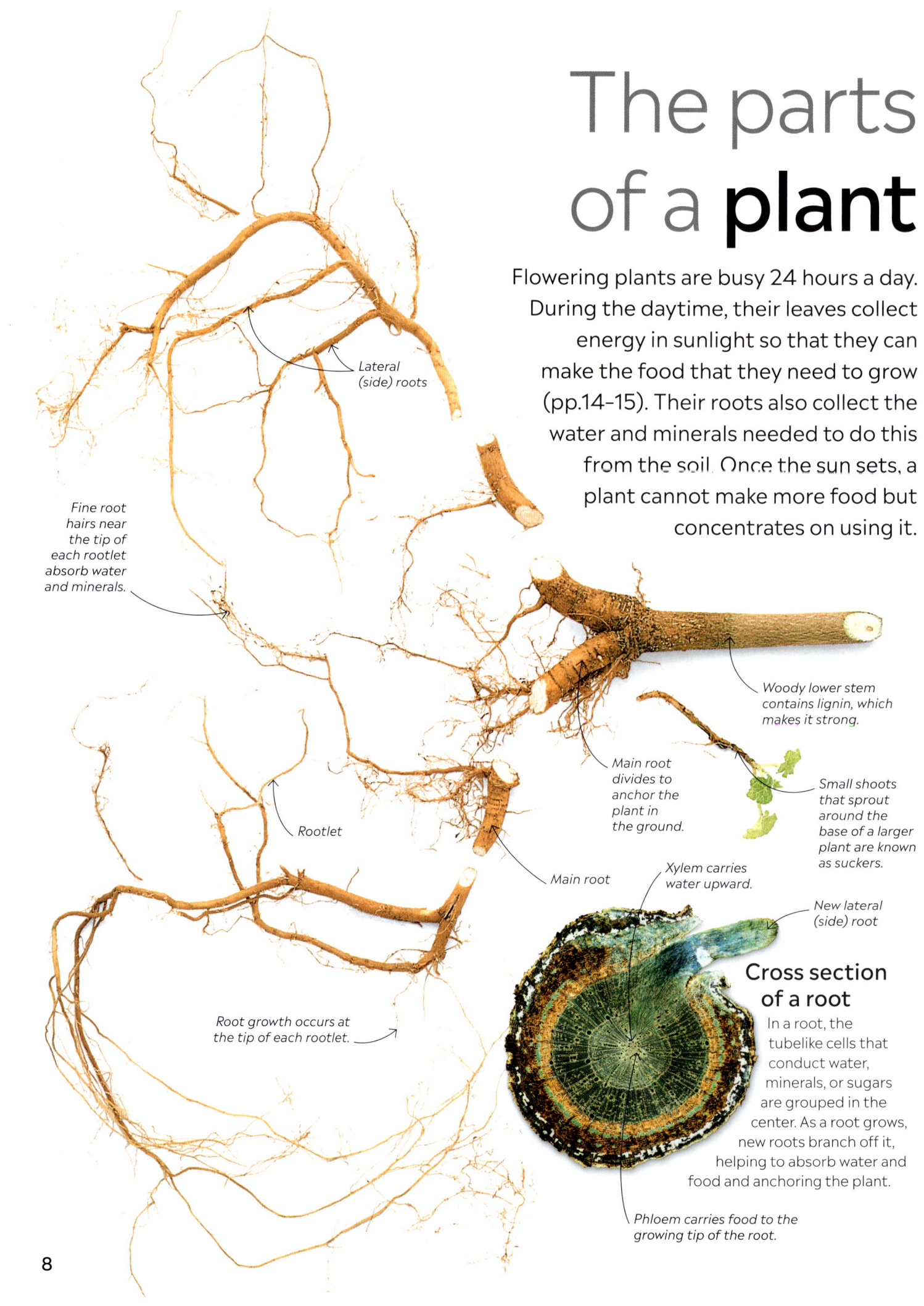

The parts of a plant

Flowering plants are busy 24 hours a day. During the daytime, their leaves collect energy in sunlight so that they can make the food that they need to grow (pp.14–15). Their roots also collect the water and minerals needed to do this from the soil. Once the sun sets, a plant cannot make more food but concentrates on using it.

Lateral (side) roots

Fine root hairs near the tip of each rootlet absorb water and minerals.

Woody lower stem contains lignin, which makes it strong.

Main root divides to anchor the plant in the ground.

Small shoots that sprout around the base of a larger plant are known as suckers.

Rootlet

Main root

Xylem carries water upward.

New lateral (side) root

Cross section of a root

In a root, the tubelike cells that conduct water, minerals, or sugars are grouped in the center. As a root grows, new roots branch off it, helping to absorb water and food and anchoring the plant.

Root growth occurs at the tip of each rootlet.

Phloem carries food to the growing tip of the root.

Phloem

Xylem

Dicot leaf: a network of veins

Midrib

Flower bud

Supply systems

Tubelike cell systems carry water, minerals, and food. Water and minerals go up through the xylem. The phloem can carry food to any part that needs it.

Axillary, or lateral (side) bud

Network of veins typical of a dicot leaf

Monocot leaf: parallel veins

Leaf veins

Flowering plants are monocots or dicots (p.66). The veins in a plant's adult leaves reveal which type it is.

Internode

Leaf node

Lateral (side) shoot grows from a bud at a leaf node.

Tree mallow

The apical bud is the one that grows at the very tip of a plant.

Petiole, or leaf stalk

Flower bud

Protective structures (sepals) cover the bud.

Sepal

EYEWITNESS

Rohit Karnik

MIT professor Rohit Karnik and his team used xylem vessels from conifers and ginkgo wood to create filters that can remove harmful bacteria from contaminated water. These tree filters are cost-effective and can improve public health in places where clean water is not accessible.

Opening bud

As the petals grow, they open to reveal the anthers (male) and stigmas (female).

Petal

Flower

The anthers produce pollen and the stigmas get ready to receive pollen (pp.22–23).

Stigmas

Anther

A plant is **born**

A seed contains an embryo from which the seedling will develop and a food supply to fuel the process of germination (growing). When conditions are right, the seed comes alive. It absorbs water, embryo cells start to divide, and eventually the seed case breaks open. The root system sprouts and grows, followed by the shoot, which will produce the stem and leaves.

First true leaves open out.

New leaves grow from the apical bud at the top of the stem.

Tiny but strong
Some seedlings exert enough pressure to push through a new road surface.

First true leaves

Shoot reaches up toward the light.

Bent first shoot (plumule)

Seed case, containing seed leaves

3 Harnessing the sun
Up to this point, growth is fueled by food in the seed leaves. But when the first true leaves open, the seedling can produce its own food by photosynthesis.

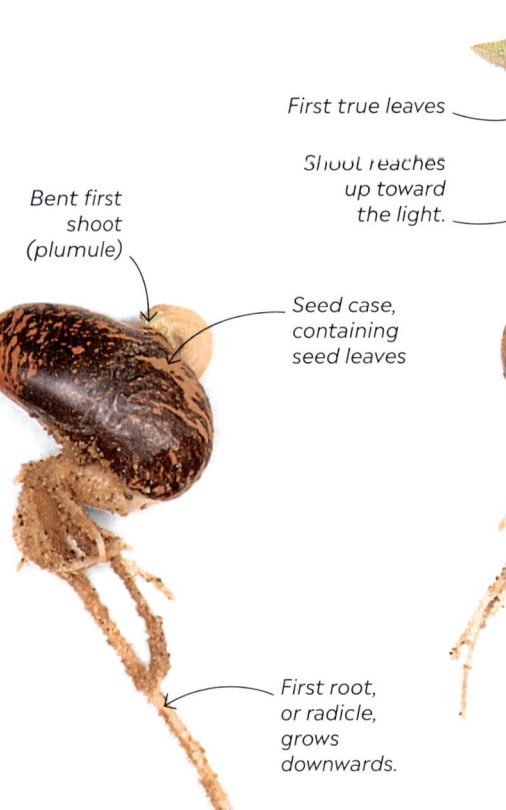

First root, or radicle, grows downwards.

1 Getting going
The seed of a scarlet runner bean will germinate only if it is dark and damp. First, the seed's skin splits. A first root, the radicle, appears, followed by a shoot. This shoot, or plumule, will produce the stem and leaves.

2 Reaching for the light
As the shoot grows longer, it breaks above ground. It straightens up toward the light, and the first true leaves appear. The bean's seed leaves stay in the seed coat, buried underground.

Main root grows deeper.

Root hairs absorb water and minerals from the soil.

*First pair of leaves,
now fully grown*

👁 **EYEWITNESS**

Michael Stausholm
Danish entrepreneur Michael Stausholm founded the company SproutWorld, which makes eco-friendly pencils with seeds inside them. When these pencils get too short, they can be put into the soil and gradually, they grow into plants, reducing waste.

*Leaf
stalk*

4 Race to reproduce

The bean plant grows fast and produces its first flowers in about six weeks. After pollination and fertilization, these will turn into pods full of seeds. When the seeds dry out, the cycle can restart.

*Slender
stem for
climbing*

Seed leaf   *Radicle*

*First leaves
emerge.*

Germinating grain

Young shoots of wheat and other grasses grow up through the soil, protected by a tube called a coleoptile. The growing point of their leaves is at ground level, so it can continue to produce new shoots at the base of the plant, even if the leaves are removed by grazing or cutting.

Coleoptile

*The seed
case is now
redundant
and starts
to shrivel.*

*Roots with
root hairs*

*Thick mass of
roots anchors
the plant.*

*Leaves develop from an
underground tuber.*

A yearly cycle

Some plants have storage organs underground. Every fall, their leaves die, but in spring new leaves develop from buds on the tuber.

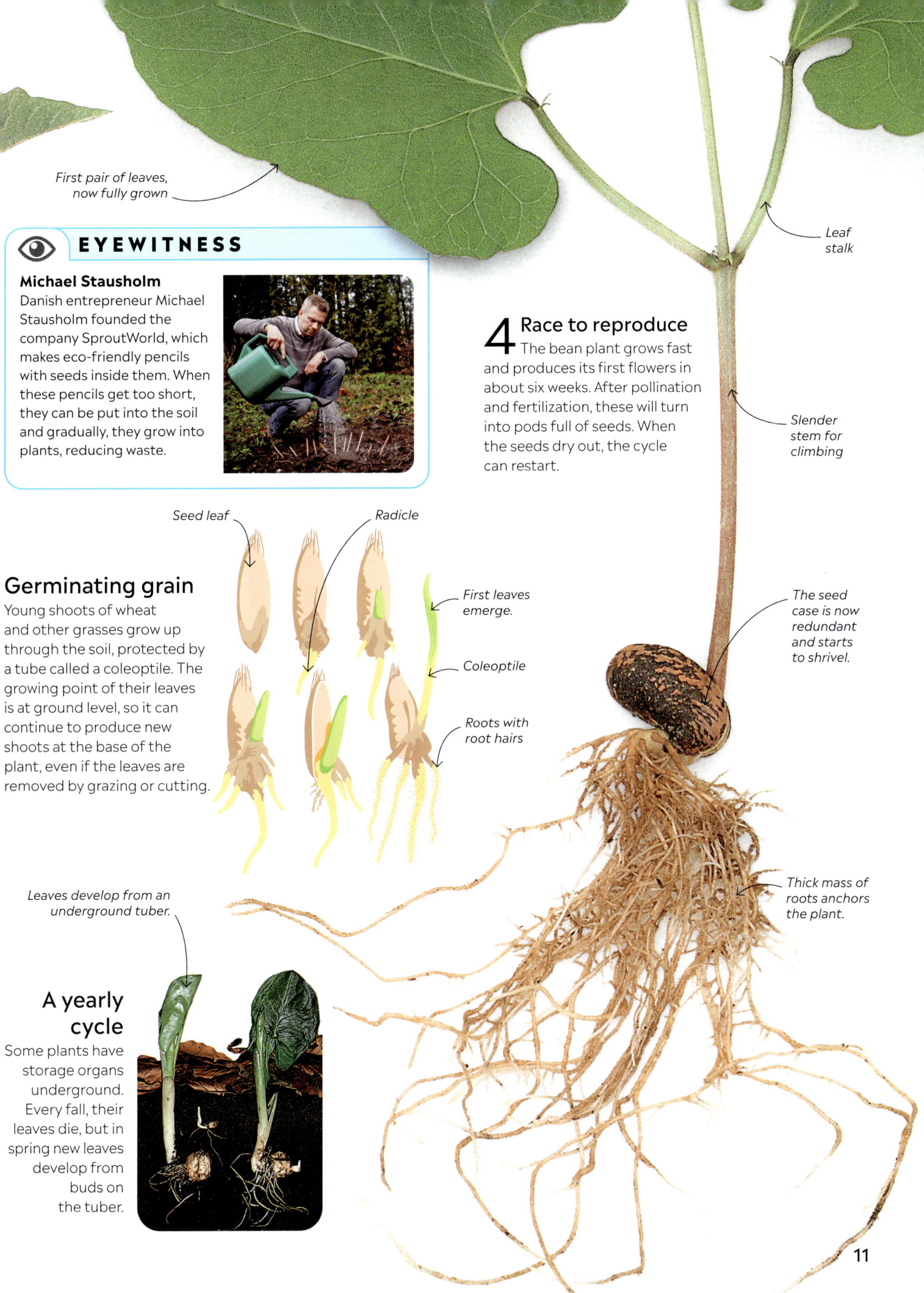

Bursting into **bloom**

All plants have triggers that make them flower at the right time. Some need warmth, and others will flower only after rain. But for many, what matters is the length of the night and day. Plants have special chemicals that sense when this alters with the seasons. Many flower when the days are getting longer. At that time of the year, the air is often filled with insects—an ideal time for flowers to be pollinated.

 EYEWITNESS

Azuma Makoto
Japanese floral artist and sculptor Azuma Makoto arranges flowers in unique ways. Makoto treats them with care and respect. He has even sent flower bouquets into the deep sea as well as to outer space.

New petals unfolding outward

Petals folded back

Sepal

Petal

The flower opens

When the light conditions are right for the garden nasturtium, flower buds begin to form. Each flower bud is protected by five sepals. As the bud bursts, the sepals open to reveal five bright orange petals that grow and fold back. One of the sepals develops a spur that produces nectar, which attracts insect pollinators.

Blooming lovely

To reach the nectar, insects have to clamber over the anthers and get covered in pollen. As the anthers wither, the stigmas get dusted by pollen from insects that have visited other plants for nectar.

The life cycles of plants

Flowering plants have different lifespans, ranging from months to centuries. Some, known as annuals, germinate, flower, set seed, and die within one year. Biennials take two years to complete the same process. Their first year is spent growing and building up food reserves, which they store in a thick root. Perennials live several years and spread vast root networks.

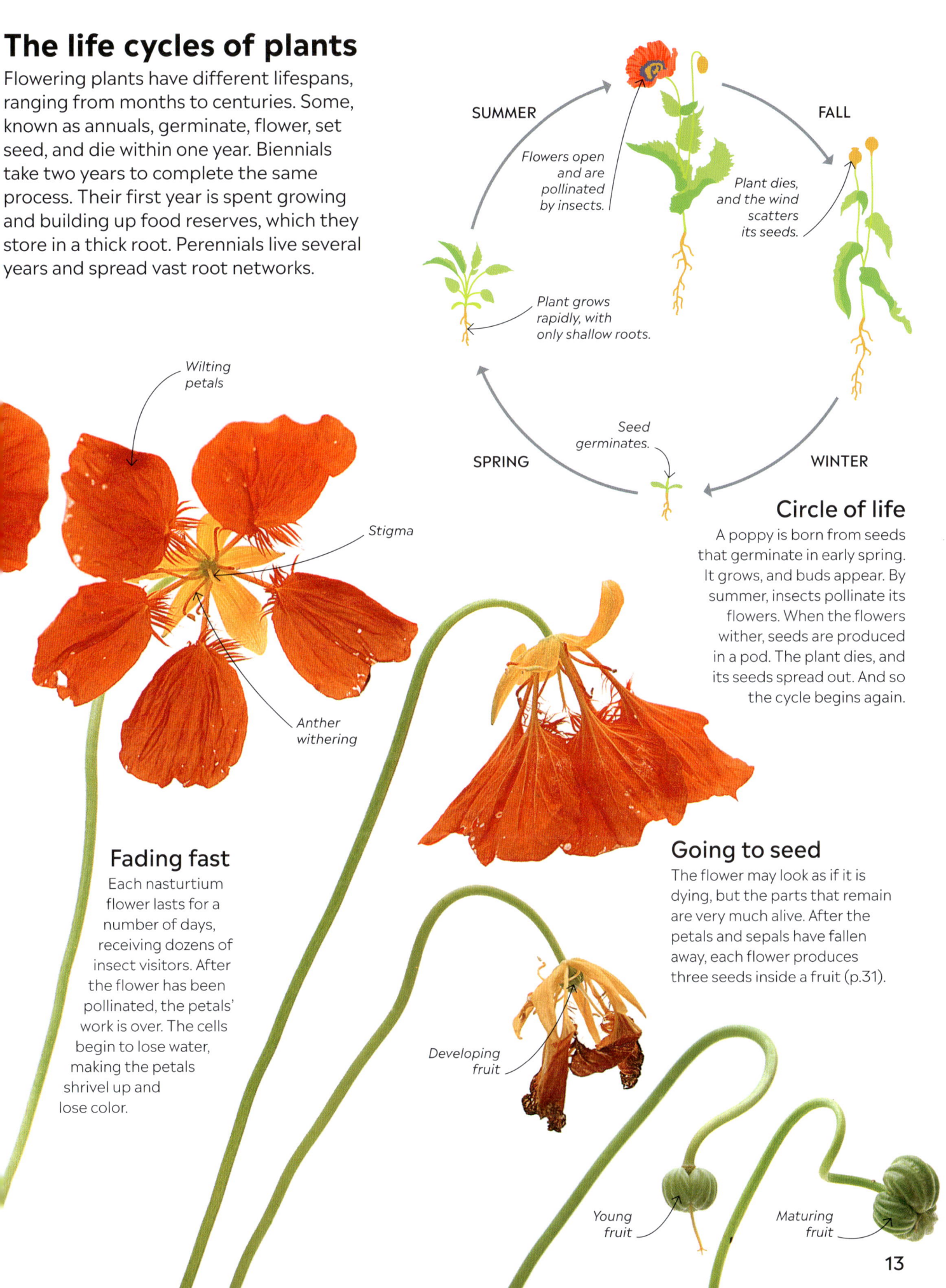

SUMMER

Flowers open and are pollinated by insects.

FALL

Plant dies, and the wind scatters its seeds.

Plant grows rapidly, with only shallow roots.

Seed germinates.

SPRING

WINTER

Wilting petals

Stigma

Anther withering

Circle of life

A poppy is born from seeds that germinate in early spring. It grows, and buds appear. By summer, insects pollinate its flowers. When the flowers wither, seeds are produced in a pod. The plant dies, and its seeds spread out. And so the cycle begins again.

Fading fast

Each nasturtium flower lasts for a number of days, receiving dozens of insect visitors. After the flower has been pollinated, the petals' work is over. The cells begin to lose water, making the petals shrivel up and lose color.

Going to seed

The flower may look as if it is dying, but the parts that remain are very much alive. After the petals and sepals have fallen away, each flower produces three seeds inside a fruit (p.31).

Developing fruit

Young fruit

Maturing fruit

13

A light diet

Plants make their own food. They use chlorophyll, a substance that makes leaves green, to trap the energy in sunlight. Then, they put the energy to work. They use it to make water combine with carbon dioxide, a gas that they get from the air. The result is glucose—an energy-rich food sugar that plants use to grow. This process is called photosynthesis. It takes in energy and uses it to build up the living parts of plants.

Underground storage

Potatoes are underground stems, known as tubers, which store food produced by photosynthesis by the potato plant. This food, in the form of starches, provides the young shoots that develop from buds on the tuber with enough fuel to enable them to grow quickly.

A plant without light

This potato has spent six months in almost complete darkness, so it has not been able to produce any food by photosynthesis. But it has grown some roots and shoots, which have drawn on the food reserves stored by the parent plant during the previous year's growth.

Leaves produced in the dark have little chlorophyll, leaving them pale.

Potato tuber kept in the dark for six months

Each stem is produced by a small bud called an eye.

Stems grow upward against gravity.

Roots that grow from stems are called adventitious roots.

Tuber begins to shrink as its food stores are used up.

Chloroplasts in cells collect sunlight.

A plant's solar panels

Inside the cells that make up a plant's leaves are tiny structures called chloroplasts. Inside the chloroplasts, the green, light-trapping pigment chlorophyll is found.

Green leaves are rich in chlorophyll.

Storing sugar

Plants store food in various ways—as starches, sugars, or oils. In its first year, an onion plant stores sugars in the onion bulb. In the second year, the sugars in the onion bulb are used up as the plant grows and flowers.

Potato tuber in light for three weeks

Rapid revival

After emerging from the dark, the potato plant is growing rapidly. Its leaves have turned green as more chlorophyll has been produced to harness sunlight. The growing potato plant can now collect enough energy to build up its own reserves, and it no longer needs the energy stored in the old tuber, which will die.

Stems rapidly grow upward and turn toward the light.

Thickening root system

15

Inside a simple flower

Flowers come in a vast array of shapes and sizes, but for seed production, all flowers use the same basic structures. The male parts (the stamens) produce the pollen, while the female parts (the carpels) include the ovary, where seeds develop. When opened up, the sepals and petals attract insects.

Simple whorl

The simplest flowers have their parts arranged in a circle, or whorl.

Stamen

Carpel

Petal from the inner whorl

Open lily flower

Sepal from the outer whorl

Lily flower bud

Sepals and petals that look the same are known as tepals.

The lily family

Lily species form one of the largest families of flowering plants.

Stamens sit tightly around the carpel.

Tepals protect the male and female parts of the flower.

How a lily flower bud opens

In the bud, the male and female parts are packed tightly together inside the protective casing made by the tepals. The bud opens because different parts of the tepals grow faster than others, for example, at the inside of their base. This forces the tepals to bend outward and open up.

Reproductive parts

The female parts, or carpels, are at the center of the flower. They include the ovary, where the seeds are produced, and the stigma, which is attached to the ovary by the style. The male parts of the flower consist of six identical stamens.

Anther produces pollen.

Filament

Stamens (male parts)

Stigma receives pollen.

Style

Ovary

Carpel (female parts)

Stamens

◉ EYEWITNESS

Neera Joshi
Nepali botanical artist Neera Joshi uses pen, ink, and watercolors to draw and paint accurate images of Himalayan plants indigenous to Nepal. Her work has been used in journals, botanical gardens, and museums to raise awareness about plant conservation.

Male and female flower parts often **mature at different times** to ensure a flower doesn't pollinate itself.

Star attraction

Surrounding the male and female parts of the lily flower is an outer ring, or whorl, of three white sepals, and an inner whorl of three white petals. In many other flowers, only the petals stand out, while the sepals that make up the outer whorl may be tough and green and protect the flower bud.

Spotted markings attract pollinating insects.

Tepals (petals and sepals) of a lily flower

A complex flower

Developing flower bud from the side

A Himalayan balsam flower has the same basic parts as the lily flower (pp.16–17), but it is much more specialized. Its nectar is produced in a spur attached to a pouch. To reach the nectar, a visiting bee first has to land on a petal platform. It then needs to climb inside the flower and stretch out its long tongue. In this position, the bee's back touches the anthers and receives a dusting of pollen, which is carried to the next flower the bee visits.

Developing nectar spur

A single Himalayan balsam plant can produce more than 2,000 seeds.

Stigma

Style

Anterior, or front, petal

Anther

Clever arrangement

When a passion flower opens, its anthers, which are closest to the nectar at its base, dust pollen onto the back of a visiting insect. A few hours later, the styles curve downward so that the stigmas are closest to the base and can collect pollen from another visitor.

Flowers develop in clusters and open one at a time.

Sepal

Pouch-shaped third sepal

Lower petals joined together

Nectar spur

Attractive features

A Himalayan balsam flower has three sepals and five petals. At its base, two of the sepals are small flaps that protect the young flower bud. The third sepal is much larger and pouch-shaped. At the end of the pouch is the spur that produces nectar.

Fully formed flower from the side

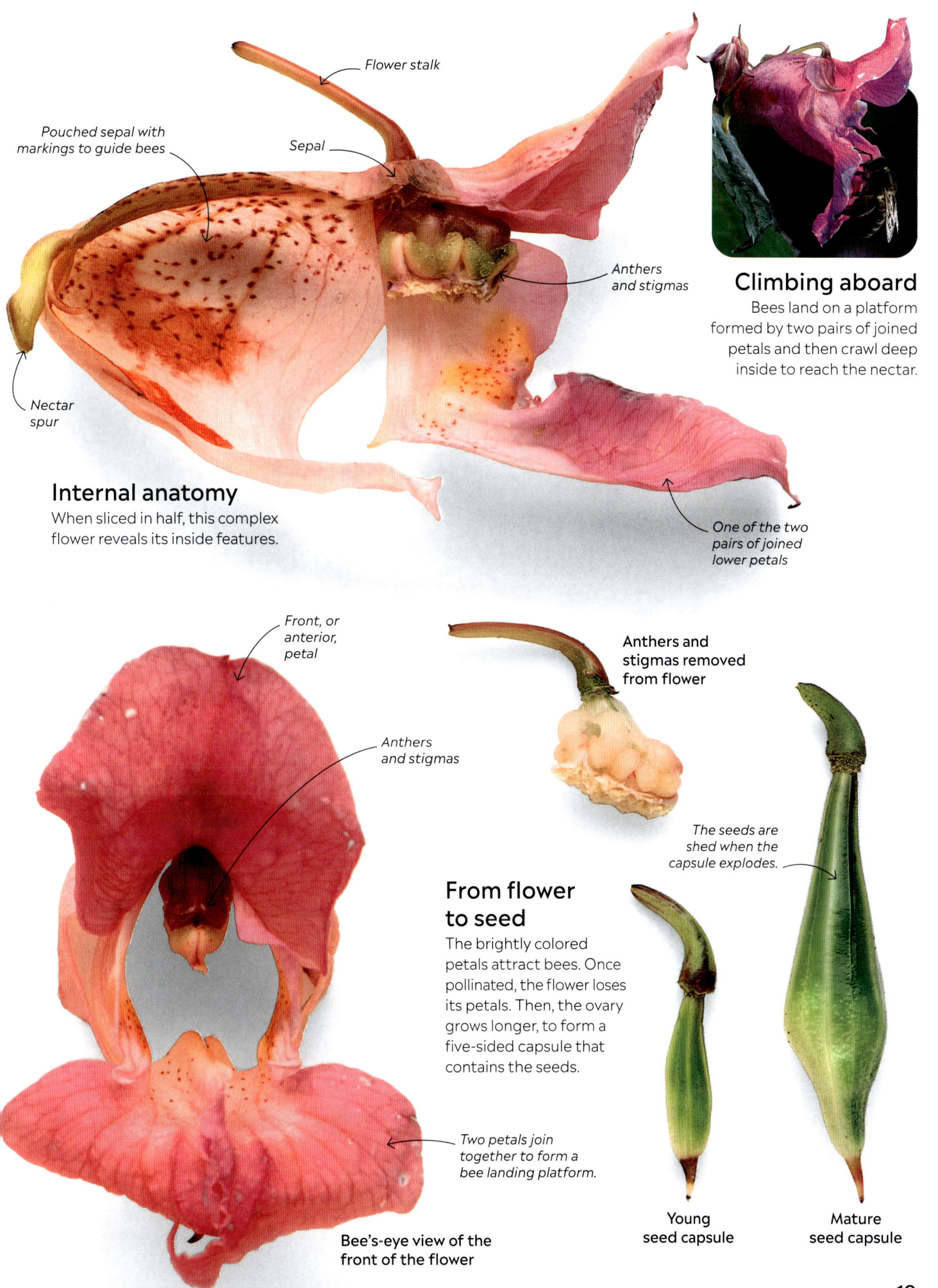

Flower stalk

Pouched sepal with markings to guide bees

Sepal

Anthers and stigmas

Nectar spur

Internal anatomy

When sliced in half, this complex flower reveals its inside features.

Climbing aboard

Bees land on a platform formed by two pairs of joined petals and then crawl deep inside to reach the nectar.

One of the two pairs of joined lower petals

Front, or anterior, petal

Anthers and stigmas

Anthers and stigmas removed from flower

The seeds are shed when the capsule explodes.

From flower to seed

The brightly colored petals attract bees. Once pollinated, the flower loses its petals. Then, the ovary grows longer, to form a five-sided capsule that contains the seeds.

Two petals join together to form a bee landing platform.

Young seed capsule

Mature seed capsule

Bee's-eye view of the front of the flower

Bear's
breeches

*Individual
flower*

Mullein

*Individual
flower*

Rosebay
willow herb

All sorts
of flowers

How many individual flowers can you see
on these pages? The answer is around
3,300—most of them too small to see without
a magnifying glass. Some plants have just a single flower.
But most of the plants shown here produce flowers
grouped together in clusters known as flower heads.
Flower heads vary in shape, size, and number of flowers.

*Petals fused
to form
a tube*

Honeysuckle

Dog rose

*Iris flowers have three
sepals, three petals,
and three stigmas.*

Iris

Regular flowers

A regular flower, such as
the dog rose, has its parts
grow in a circular plan.

Flower spires

Flowers in spires usually open
in sequence, starting at the
bottom. It may take weeks
before the top buds open.

Sepal

Irregular
flowers

Most irregular
flowers, such as
the sweet pea,
can be divided
into two halves
that are mirror images
of each other.

Petal

Sweet
pea

Clematis

Bright purple tepal

Showy tepals

The clematis has six brightly colored tepals (identical petals and sepals).

Ray floret has a single ray.

White ray florets

Disc floret with outer ray florets removed

Disc florets

Eryngo has dome-shaped flower clusters.

Clusters resemble thistle heads.

Chamomile, part of the daisy family

Hogweed has typical umbrella-shaped flower clusters.

Composite flowers

Sunflowers, daisies, and other composite flowers have flower heads made up of two types of florets—disc florets and ray florets. The tiny composite flower heads of the yarrow sit together in clusters.

Sunflower

Eryngo

Flowers in umbels

Tiny flowers are easier for pollinating insects to spot and land on when they grow together in clusters known as umbels.

Hogweed

Cluster of flower heads

Cultivated yarrow

How a plant is pollinated

Some plants are able to pollinate themselves, but most need pollen from another plant of the same species (cross-pollination). Pollen can travel by wind or water, but insects are the most important pollinators. Plants entice insects to their flowers by their bright colors and by food in the form of nectar. Bees come to collect pollen for themselves, too. Some flowers are pollinated by a wide range of insects, while others rely on just one species to do the job.

Family home
Worker honey bees bring nectar and pollen back to the hive to feed their developing young.

Pollen basket on bee's hind leg

Honeyguide

Floral feeding station
Honeyguides on the flower guide the bee to the nectar. As the bees feed on the nectar, they also collect pollen in baskets on their legs, to be carried back to their nest.

Bright yellow guide marks show bees where to land.

Petal acting as a landing platform

Opening up
When a bumblebee lands on a common toadflax flower, the flower's throat is closed. To reach the nectar inside, the bee must push through.

Nectar tube

Climbing in
As the bumblebee crawls over the hump that seals the flower's throat, it picks up pollen as it brushes against the anthers inside the flower.

Feeding time
Any pollen the bee is already carrying sticks to the stigma, and the flower is pollinated.

Flowers of the fly orchid

The real thing!

Female impersonators

Some orchids use tricks to ensure they are pollinated. Their flowers look and smell so much like a female fly, wasp, or bee that males try to mate with them. Pollen sticks to the visitor's body and is carried to the next flower.

Pollen grains

The largest pollen grains measure only about 1/120 in (0.2 mm) across, and they have very intricate shapes.

Pollen grains magnified many times to show the variety of shapes

Short proboscis

Long proboscis

Drinking straws

Butterflies and moths suck up nectar through the proboscis, which is hollow like a drinking straw.

Butterfly pollination

Butterflies have a great sense of smell, so butterfly-pollinated flowers are often scented. Many plants flower in late summer, when lots of butterflies flutter from flower to flower in search of nectar and help disperse pollen as they go.

Pollen sticks to the butterfly's wings and body.

Marjoram

Continued from previous page

Curious pollinators

Many plant species depend on pollinators other than bees and butterflies. They are highly adapted to attract specific animals, using foul smells to draw in flies or bright colors as signals to birds. A few have clever mechanisms to trap visitors, who escape only once covered in pollen.

Australian western underground orchid

Disappearing trick

One orchid spends almost all of its life underground. Appearing briefly, level with the surface, its flowers attract gnats and termites that help spread their pollen.

Cultivated fly-pollinated orchid

Hairs on the petals attract insects.

Shiny surface appeals to flies.

Smelly attraction

Flies are attracted by the smell of decaying flesh, so many flowers that rely on flies for pollination have a putrid odor. This orchid even has hairs on its petals to give it an animal-like feel. The shiny surface also tempts flies.

Flowers are lilac at first but turn red as they open.

Pink bracts attract birds.

Flowers appear among the bracts.

Urn plant

Red signal

This urn plant grows on trees and needs to stand out to get pollinators' attention. Birds have excellent color vision, and red or pink flowers signal "come here for nectar."

A brush for birds

Many species of hibiscus are pollinated by hummingbirds. A hummingbird hovers in front of the flower and inserts its long beak deep inside to reach the nectar. As it feeds, the anthers brush pollen onto its head, while the stigma, also brushing its head, collects pollen from another flower.

Brushlike anthers

Hibiscus flower

Bizarre beauty

The yellow calla lily is pollinated by fungus gnats. The insects crawl down to the base, where they become trapped by hairs. As they move around, they deposit and pick up pollen. The hairs wither, and the insects crawl out again, ready to move on.

Bright yellow spathe (leaflike hood) envelops the male and female flowers on the spadix, or central spike.

Yellow calla lily

Possum pollination

The Australian honey possum lives entirely on the pollen and nectar of flowers such as this banksia. It collects its food with its long snout and brushlike tongue.

Translucent, window-like cells let in light.

Trapped flies try to escape by flying up toward the light and become covered with pollen.

Flies fall down this hollow tube and are trapped by downward-pointing hairs.

Landing flap

Taking prisoners

This flower smells of rotting fish. Eager flies enter it and get trapped overnight. When the flower withers, the pollen-covered flies can escape.

Brazilian birthwort

Colorful lobe (rounded projection) attracts flies.

A redwing may help spread the apples' seeds.

Winter feast

Many animals rely on fruit for food and may help spread a fruit's seeds.

Making seeds

Plants grow flowers to make seeds and spread them to grow in new places. Once pollination (pp.22–23) has taken place, the male pollen grain grows a tiny tube down through the female part of the flower. Here, it searches out a female cell, or ovule, to fertilize. The fertilized ovule starts to turn into a seed and then into a fruit. The fruit will help the seeds to spread. Some plants produce fruits that attract animals who scatter the seeds as they feed. Others produce dry, hard fruits. Their seeds are spread by other means (pp.28–29).

Sepals protect the bud.

Receptacle containing ovaries and ovules

Early days

The beginnings of the rose hip sit at the top of the stem, attached to the flower parts. Known as the receptacle, it holds the rose's female parts – the ovaries and ovules.

The Rose of Hildesheim in Germany is thought to be more than 1,000 years old.

Petals open out.

Rose in bloom

The bud opens into a flower, attracting bees for pollination. Once the flower has been pollinated and the ovules fertilized, the receptacle begins to swell.

Green sepals fold back.

Thorns keep leaf-eating animals away.

Slow transformation

After fertilization, the ovule begins to change into a fruit. The petals, no longer needed to attract bees, wither and fall off.

Swelling receptacle

Dried-up stamens

Withering petal

Stamen

Sepal

Inside story

The receptacle is full of ovaries. Each ovary contains an ovule, which requires its own pollen grain for fertilization. The fertilized ovule develops into a seed.

Seed, surrounded by an ovary

Cutaway diagram of a receptacle

The rose hip

As the fertilized ovules turn into seeds, the receptacle swells and goes red. When it is ripe, it is called a rose hip.

Swollen receptacle starts to change color.

Wasted work

Some birds peck out the rose hip's seeds and crack them open to get to the nutrients inside. The seeds are destroyed instead of becoming dispersed by the bird's droppings.

Fruit is rich in vitamin C.

Useful fruits

Rose hips contain vitamin C, good for animals and people.

Fair exchange

Birds and other animals eat the fruit and spread the seeds in their droppings.

Cross section of a ripe rose hip

Hairy seeds

Bright red fruit attracts birds.

Precious cargo

The seeds inside have tough skins and are covered in short hairs. This helps the seeds travel through a bird's digestive tract intact.

Sepal

Sepals dry out and shrivel up.

Agrimony

How seeds are **spread**

Plants have evolved some very effective ways of spreading their seeds so they end up somewhere they can germinate. Some plants use exploding seed pods. Others have flying or floating seeds or fruits, or fruits that stick to animals passing by.

Lotus seed heads

Seed held in a cup

Each fruit has many tiny spines.

Fruits with hooks

Dried lotus seed head, seen from above

Washed away
The lotus is a water plant. When its seeds are ripe, they fall and float away. They can germinate more than 200 years later.

Lesser burdock

Hitching a lift
Fruits with spines and hooks, known as burrs, cling to the fur of passing animals. When burrs are scratched or rubbed off, the seeds fall to the ground.

Burrs on the fur on a dog's back

👁 EYEWITNESS

George de Mestral
This Swiss engineer accidentally discovered the secret to Velcro® in the 1940s. While taking a walk, he found cockleburs stuck to his trousers. On examining the burrs, he found they had tiny hooks that latched onto the fabric. He used this principle to create a fastener for clothes.

Off to a flying start

Some plants disperse their seeds with natural catapults. The tension built up as the seed case grows is released and the case splits open, flinging seeds in all directions.

Closed seed pod

When touched, the seed case curls up and the seeds are flicked out.

Unexploded seed pod

Himalayan balsam flower

Seeds of meadow cranesbill are catapulted out.

Tiny, light seeds

Columbine

Blowing in the wind

When the wind shakes the seed heads of an opium poppy or a columbine, seeds are scattered near the parent plant. Thistle fruits (with seeds inside) catch the wind, traveling much farther.

Seeds are sprinkled.

Pods of tufted vetch snap open when dry.

Intact pod

Fruits with parachutes are carried by the wind.

Opium poppy

Shunning the light

The ivy-leaved toadflax pushes its seed heads into rock crevices. Here, the seeds can germinate away from the light.

Creeping thistle

Borne on the **wind**

The dandelion's flower is a composite flower head made up of many tiny florets (p.21). Each of the florets produces a single tiny fruit. Inside each fruit, a seed will grow and, when ready, develop a feathery parachute to help it float through the air. If you blow a fluffy dandelion clock, you'll set the seeds off in the same way as the wind does.

Petals in open flower head

1 Opening time
The dandelion's flower opens in the morning, waiting to be pollinated by insects. It closes in the afternoon and when it begins to rain.

Dandelion fruits floating away on the breeze

Flower closes before the seeds form.

Bracts protect the developing seed head.

2 Seeds start to form
After opening and closing for days, the pollinated flower shuts, and seed formation begins. Gradually, the petals wither away, and the pappus (the small circle of hairs attached to the top of each fruit) starts to grow.

Seed head opens when the parachutes are formed.

Bracts fold back.

Fully opened seed head

3 Opening out

The seed head opens when the weather is dry. The parachutes are squashed together, but as the bracts around the seed head fold back, the parachutes expand.

4 Ready to go

Without wind, the fruits stay on the seed head. At this point, seed-eating birds might peck them off.

Parachutes attached to tiny fruits

5 Lift off

A slightest breeze is all that is needed to lift the parachutes into the air. When they land, the parachutes break off and the seeds sink into the soil, waiting for spring to come before they germinate.

Spreading without **seeds**

Some plants reproduce by turning small pieces of themselves into new plants. This is known as vegetative reproduction. When a plant reproduces in this way, the young plantlets are genetically identical to the parent. This is useful for farmers and gardeners, as they can multiply good plants that produce tasty fruit or attractive flowers.

Creeping buttercup

Parent plant

Creeping stems

Stolons are stems that stretch along the ground. New plants grow from buds forming on the stems. As the plants set root, the stems wither away.

Piggyback plant

Tiny piggyback plantlets grow at the base of the older leaves and look as though they are having a piggyback ride.

Fallen plantlets

Runner, known as stolon

Strawberry plant

Parent plant

Bud at a leaf node

Chandelier plant

Leaf tip plantlets

Succulents (p.53) develop tiny plantlets along their leaves or, like this chandelier plant, just at the tips. When mature, plantlets fall off and take root in the soil.

Growing strawberries

Strawberry plants reproduce using runners from which new plants grow and root. Berry farmers can cut the runner and transplant the new plant.

A myth exploded

Uprooted by the wind, tumbleweeds blow across the prairies of North America. The dead plants can't put down roots but spread by seeds scattered as they tumble.

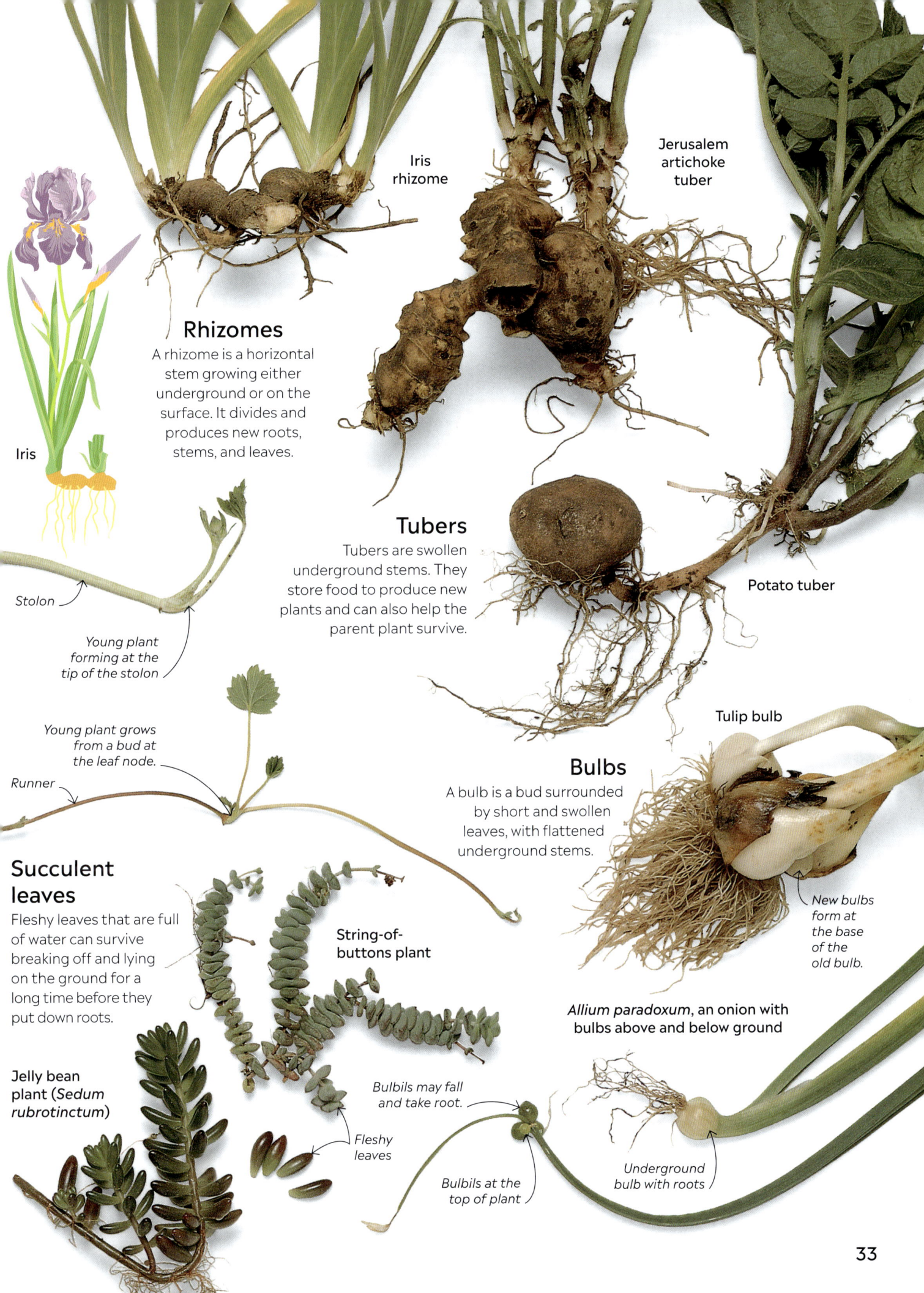

Iris
rhizome

Jerusalem
artichoke
tuber

Rhizomes

A rhizome is a horizontal stem growing either underground or on the surface. It divides and produces new roots, stems, and leaves.

Iris

Stolon

Young plant forming at the tip of the stolon

Tubers

Tubers are swollen underground stems. They store food to produce new plants and can also help the parent plant survive.

Potato tuber

Tulip bulb

Young plant grows from a bud at the leaf node.

Runner

Bulbs

A bulb is a bud surrounded by short and swollen leaves, with flattened underground stems.

New bulbs form at the base of the old bulb.

Succulent leaves

Fleshy leaves that are full of water can survive breaking off and lying on the ground for a long time before they put down roots.

String-of-buttons plant

Allium paradoxum, an onion with bulbs above and below ground

Jelly bean plant (*Sedum rubrotinctum*)

Bulbils may fall and take root.

Fleshy leaves

Bulbils at the top of plant

Underground bulb with roots

Living leaves

Leaves are so varied because each species of plant faces its own challenges in harvesting sunlight (pp.14–15). A plant living on the gloomy floor of a rainforest may need big leaves to catch enough light. A plant growing on top of a cliff has plenty of light, but it is lashed by strong winds, so it needs small, strong leaves to survive. Some plants have more than one type of leaf.

Water plants

Feathery water-plant leaves allow water to flow past without causing them damage.

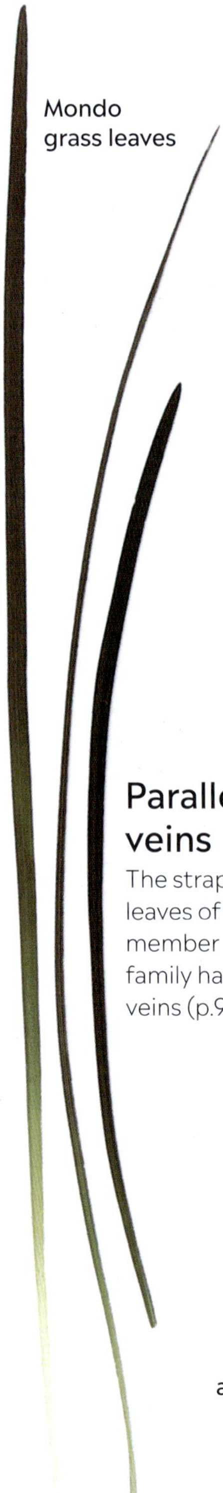

Mondo grass leaves

Color change

The leaves of herb Robert change from green to crimson as fall approaches.

Pyrethrum

Parallel veins

The straplike leaves of this member of the lily family have parallel veins (p.9).

Furry leaves

Some leaves have a furlike covering that helps reduce water loss.

Older leaves

Young leaves

Different shapes

The leaves on young eucalyptus stems are round and encircle the stem. Older stem parts have long leaves growing on stalks.

Facing the wind

Wild asparagus lives on windy coasts. Its feathery leaflike stems can withstand gales.

Wild asparagus

Waterside giants

Gunnera leaves can be enormous, growing up to 6 ft (2 m) in diameter.

Underside of a part of a gunnera leaf

Rowan leaf

Leaflet

Compound leaf
These leaves consist of many small leaflets.

Grapefruit tree leaf

Slashed leaves
Some plants grow leaves with slashes or holes. One of these is the monstera, also known as the Swiss cheese plant.

Simple leaf
Leaves without leaflets are called simple leaves.

Slashes appear as the leaf grows older.

Nasturtium leaf

Peltate leaf
A peltate leaf is circular with a stalk in the middle.

Waxy upper surface

Evergreen leaves
Evergreen plants do not lose their leaves in winter, so their leaves need to be tough to survive several years of wind, sun, and rain.

Joseph's coat

Rhododendron leaves

Lungwort

Some varieties have red undersides.

Downy underside

Leaves of many colors
Variegated, or multicolored, leaves are often found in garden plants.

Self-defense

Plants have evolved special weapons and armor to protect themselves from being eaten. Their attackers range from tiny insects that suck sap or chew their way through leaves, to large mammals that eat entire plants. Some plants have fine hairs on their leaves to keep tiny creatures at bay, while spines, thorns, and stings deter larger ones. As a final defense, many plants release unpleasant chemicals.

Thorns grow in pairs.

Hole through which ants enter the thorn

Dried acacia twig

Bulbous thorn

Ant

Ants on guard

Some acacia trees get help from stinging ants to keep browsers away. In return, the ants get to eat the sweet pith of the swollen thorns and turn them into hollow shelters.

Barbs along the edge of the leaf

Sharp tip of a nettle sting, magnified many times

Long, sharp spines

Small, fleshy leaves

Running into trouble

Screw pines have tough, sword-shaped leaves. Rows of vicious barbs line edges and midribs, impaling any animal that gets too close.

Alluaudia

Protected leaves

In hot, dry climates, leaves are a key source of food and water for animals. This plant's spines are longer than its leaves, so it is hard for animals to get to the leaves.

Chemical warfare

When touched, a nettle's sting cells release a cocktail of chemicals that cause painful irritation. Animals remember the sting and avoid the nettle.

Barbs along the midrib

Nettle

Screw pine leaf

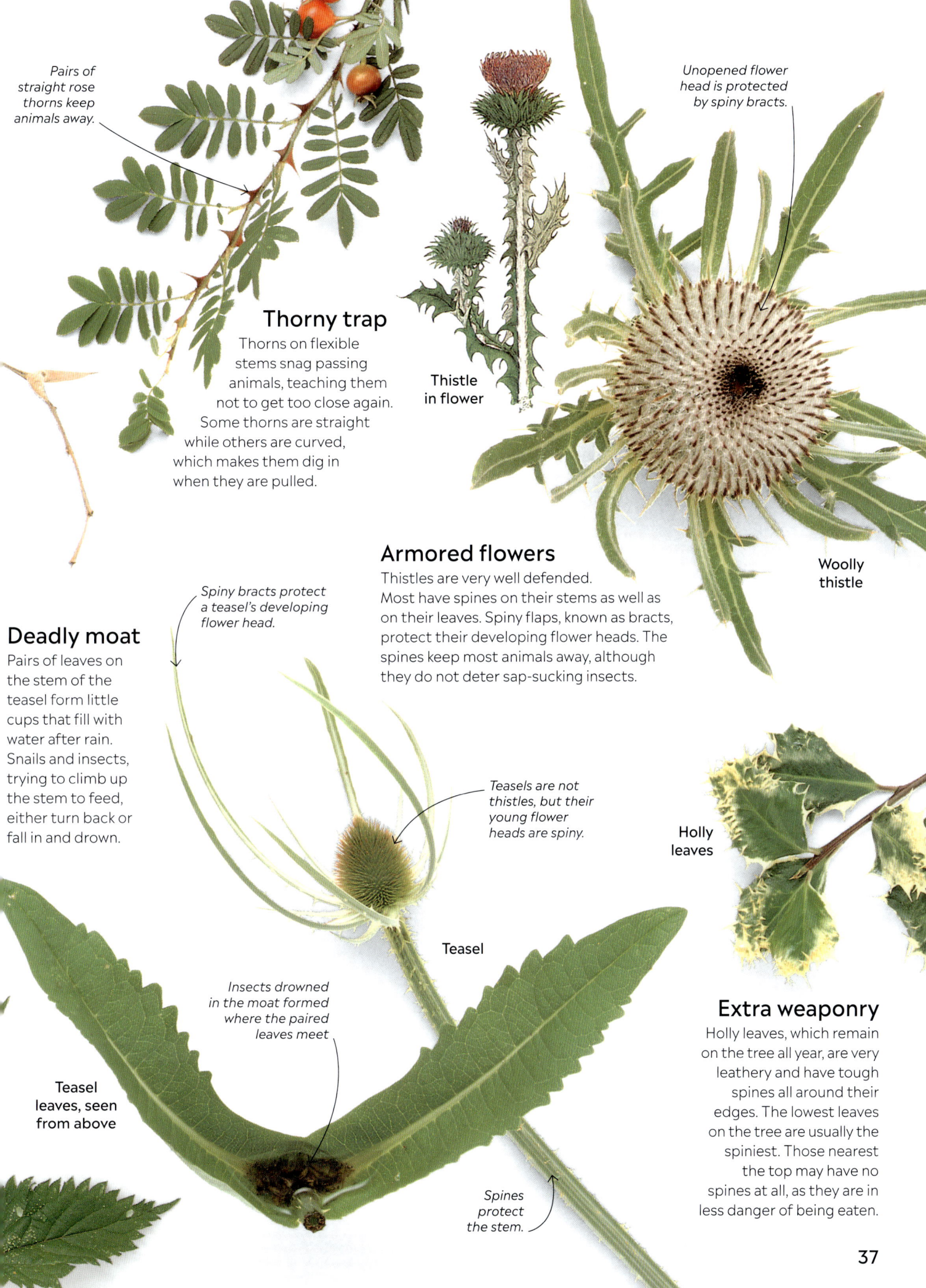

Pairs of straight rose thorns keep animals away.

Unopened flower head is protected by spiny bracts.

Thorny trap

Thorns on flexible stems snag passing animals, teaching them not to get too close again. Some thorns are straight while others are curved, which makes them dig in when they are pulled.

Thistle in flower

Woolly thistle

Armored flowers

Thistles are very well defended. Most have spines on their stems as well as on their leaves. Spiny flaps, known as bracts, protect their developing flower heads. The spines keep most animals away, although they do not deter sap-sucking insects.

Spiny bracts protect a teasel's developing flower head.

Deadly moat

Pairs of leaves on the stem of the teasel form little cups that fill with water after rain. Snails and insects, trying to climb up the stem to feed, either turn back or fall in and drown.

Teasels are not thistles, but their young flower heads are spiny.

Teasel

Holly leaves

Teasel leaves, seen from above

Insects drowned in the moat formed where the paired leaves meet

Spines protect the stem.

Extra weaponry

Holly leaves, which remain on the tree all year, are very leathery and have tough spines all around their edges. The lowest leaves on the tree are usually the spiniest. Those nearest the top may have no spines at all, as they are in less danger of being eaten.

Creepers and **climbers**

When plants grow densely together, they struggle against each other for light. The tallest gets the greatest share but spends a lot of energy growing a strong stem to hold up its leaves. Climber plants take a short cut to the top. They use other plants, and even buildings, to get a place in the light with much less effort. Some twine themselves around a neighbor, while others send out tendrils searching for support or climb by means of their own stiff side roots.

Spiraling growth
Plants that grow in a spiral will twist in a set direction. Viewed from below, scarlet runner bean plants twist clockwise.

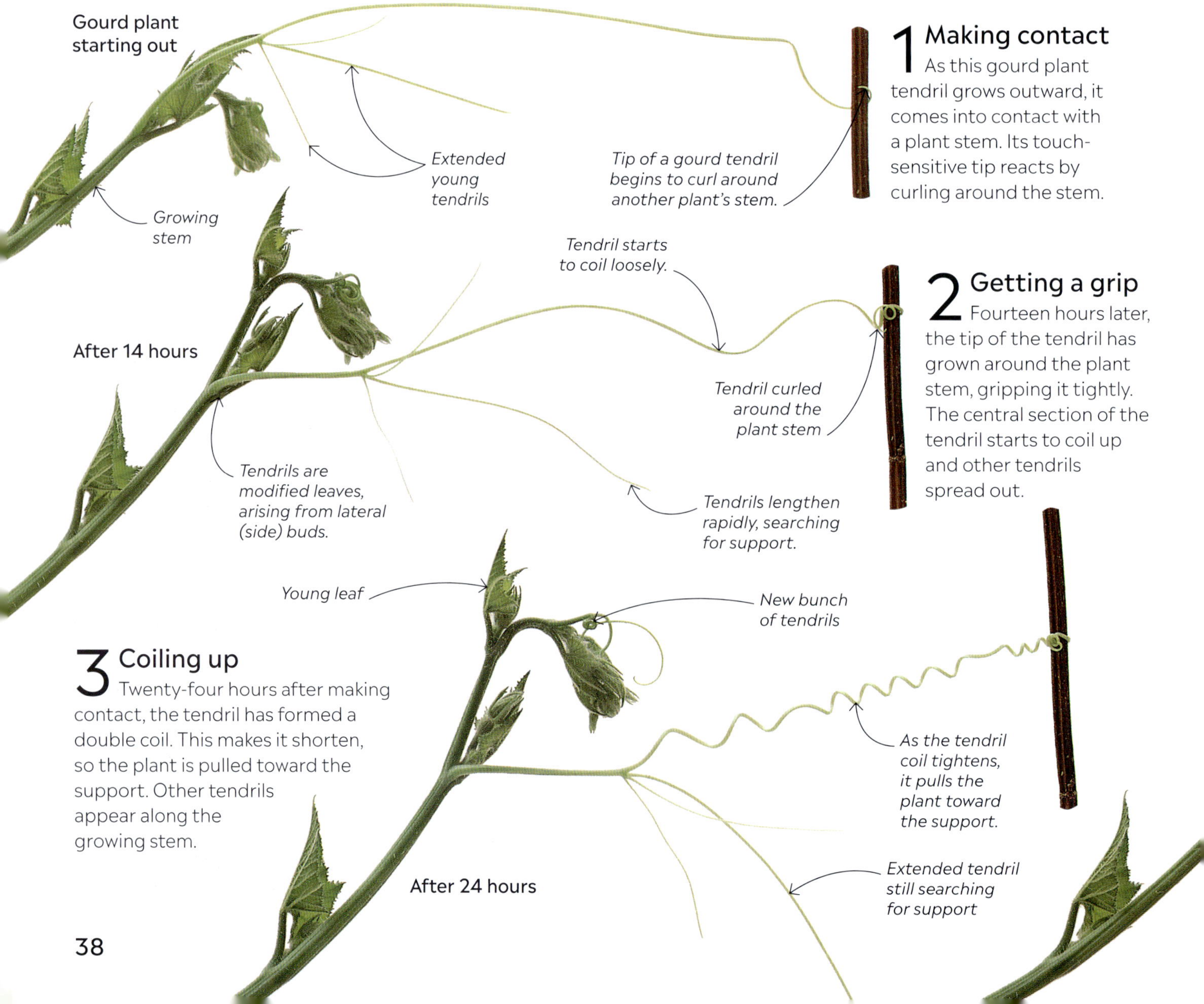

Gourd plant starting out

Extended young tendrils

Growing stem

Tip of a gourd tendril begins to curl around another plant's stem.

1 Making contact
As this gourd plant tendril grows outward, it comes into contact with a plant stem. Its touch-sensitive tip reacts by curling around the stem.

After 14 hours

Tendril starts to coil loosely.

Tendril curled around the plant stem

Tendrils are modified leaves, arising from lateral (side) buds.

Tendrils lengthen rapidly, searching for support.

2 Getting a grip
Fourteen hours later, the tip of the tendril has grown around the plant stem, gripping it tightly. The central section of the tendril starts to coil up and other tendrils spread out.

Young leaf

New bunch of tendrils

3 Coiling up
Twenty-four hours after making contact, the tendril has formed a double coil. This makes it shorten, so the plant is pulled toward the support. Other tendrils appear along the growing stem.

As the tendril coil tightens, it pulls the plant toward the support.

After 24 hours

Extended tendril still searching for support

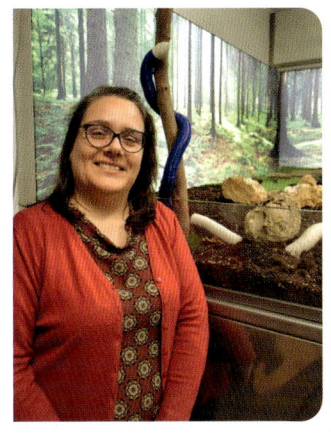

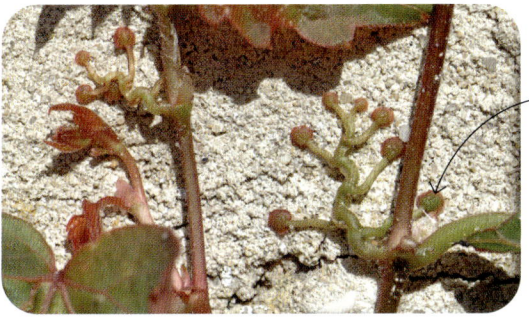

EYEWITNESS

Emanuela Del Dottore
Italian researcher Del Dottore built a plantlike climbing robot called FiloBot, as part of a project coordinated by Dr Barbara Mazzolai at the Istituto Italiano di Tecnologia. It has sensors at its tip and 3D prints itself to grow like many twining plants. The robot can also collect data from hard-to-reach places, such as treetops.

Suckerlike pads

Sticking pads

Some members of the grape vine family have tendrils with small, suckerlike pads at the tip. These stick to other plants or walls.

The climber kudzu can grow 1 ft (30 cm) per day.

---

4 Making fast

Forty-eight hours after making contact, the plant is securely supported by more than one tendril.

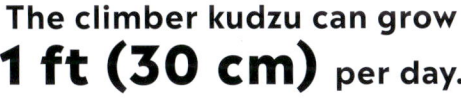

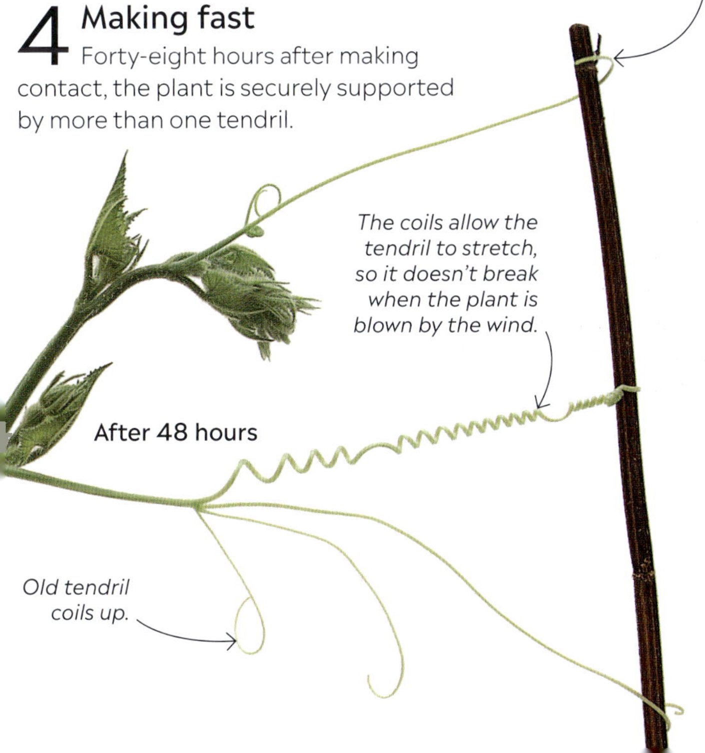
Next tendril makes contact higher up this plant stem.
The coils allow the tendril to stretch, so it doesn't break when the plant is blown by the wind.
After 48 hours
Old tendril coils up.

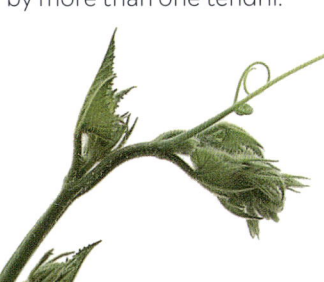

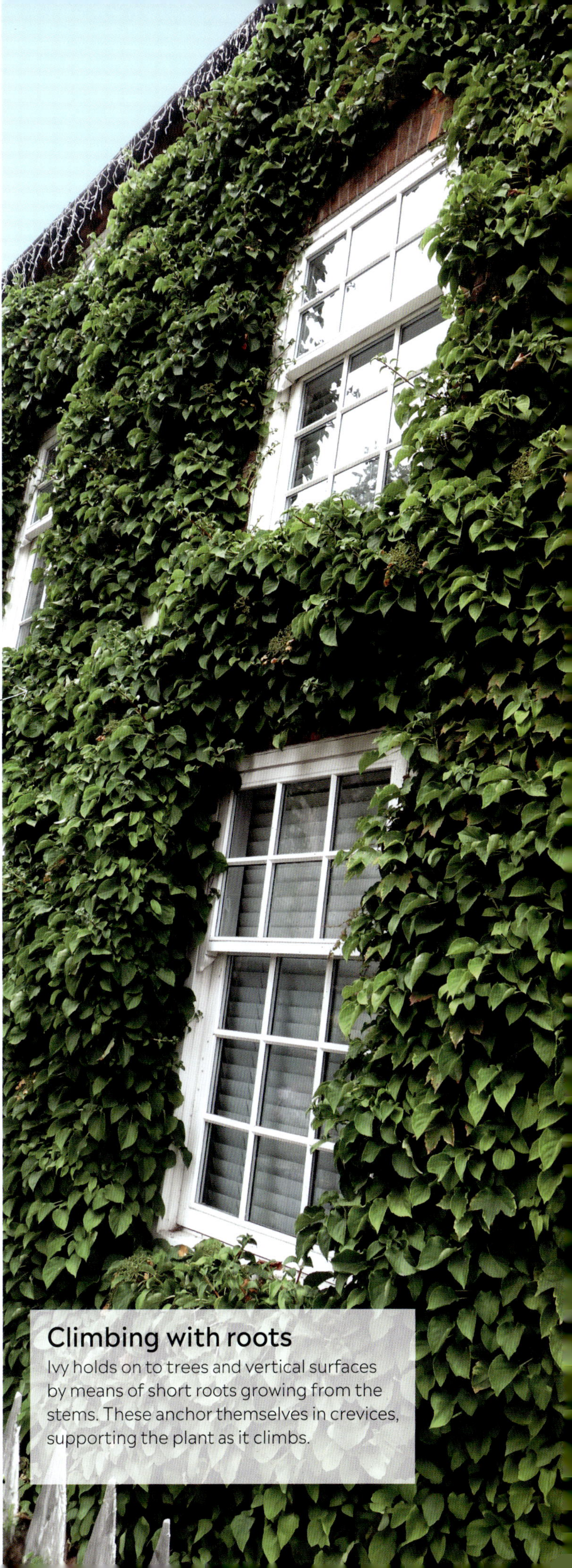
House wall covered with ivy

Climbing with roots

Ivy holds on to trees and vertical surfaces by means of short roots growing from the stems. These anchor themselves in crevices, supporting the plant as it climbs.

Meat eaters

Carnivorous plants eat insects. Some species, such as the Venus flytrap (pp.42–43), have active traps with moving parts. Others trap insects that land on them on a sticky surface or drown them in a pool of fluid. The caught insect is slowly dissolved by digestive fluids produced by the plant. After many days, all that is left is the insect's exoskeleton—the hard outer casing of the body. The rest has been absorbed. Insects add essential food to these plants, which grow in water-logged soil that is poor in nutrients.

Tendril extending from leaf holds the pitcher.

Rim

Useful leaves
People once used to hang up sticky Portuguese sundew leaves indoors, to catch flies.

Flower of the Cape sundew

Hanging traps
There are more than 100 species of insect-eating hanging pitcher plants, or nepenthes.

Sticky hairs
Sundew leaves are covered in hairs that produce droplets of glue. When an insect lands, it gets stuck to the hairs, which then fold over and trap it.

Fly trapped by hairs on a sundew leaf

Water flea trapped in bubblelike bladder

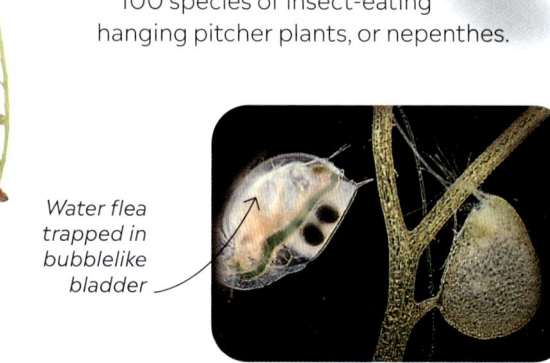

Water traps
Bladderworts use bladders as traps. When a small aquatic animal swims past, the bladder snaps open and sucks it in.

Lying in wait
Butterworts have circles of flat, sticky leaves. Any insect stuck to the surface eventually dies. The leaf edges gradually curl inward, and the insect is digested.

Cape sundew

Leaf covered with short, sticky hairs

Butterwort

Hanging nepenthes pitcher

Rim where nectar is produced

A scene from the 18th century depicting hanging nepenthes pitcher plants

Frilly rim

Leaf of a hanging pitcher plant

Death in the swamps

American pitcher plants catch their food in the same way as the hanging pitcher plants, but instead of hanging from leaves, their pitchers grow up from the ground.

Waxy scales inside the pitcher stop insects from climbing back up.

Lid prevents too much rain from diluting the liquid kept at the bottom.

Cobra lily

Insects that enter a cobra lily are confused by light that shines in through special cells in its roof. They fly toward the light again and again, become exhausted, drop into the liquid, and drown.

Patches of translucent cells

Deadly downfall

The traps of hanging pitcher plants are like jugs. Insects are lured to the pitcher by its bright color, as well as by the sweet nectar produced around its rim. They lose their footing on the slippery rim and fall inside, drowning in the digestive fluid at the bottom, which then breaks them down.

These insects are being digested slowly in the fluid that collects at the bottom of the pitcher.

Nectar lures in insects here.

Vertical cross section of a hanging pitcher

American pitcher plants

Cobra lily, or California pitcher plant

41

Snappy trap

To an insect, the tip of a Venus flytrap leaf appears to be a safe landing place. But as soon as the insect touches two or more bristles, the leaf tip springs to life with lightning speed and its two halves snap shut. The plant tests what it has caught using sensory glands. If the prey contains protein, the trap closes fully, and digestion begins. The trap is a clever device. If just one bristle is touched, by a raindrop, for example, the trap stays open.

A Venus flytrap may take
five to **12 days**
to digest its prey.

Marginal teeth

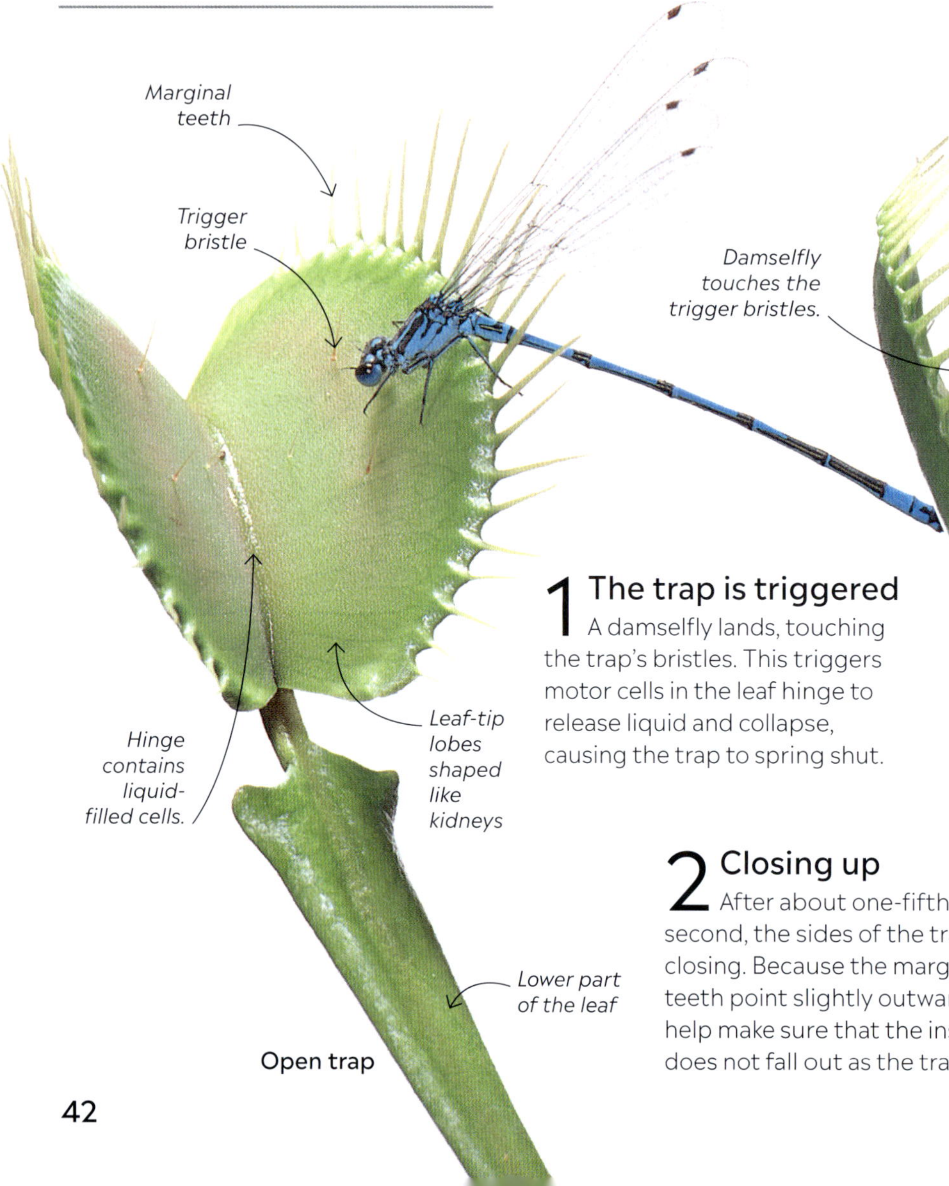

Trigger bristle

Damselfly touches the trigger bristles.

Damselfly is caught in the closing trap.

Hinge contains liquid-filled cells.

Leaf-tip lobes shaped like kidneys

1 The trap is triggered
A damselfly lands, touching the trap's bristles. This triggers motor cells in the leaf hinge to release liquid and collapse, causing the trap to spring shut.

2 Closing up
After about one-fifth of a second, the sides of the trap are closing. Because the marginal teeth point slightly outward, they help make sure that the insect does not fall out as the trap shuts.

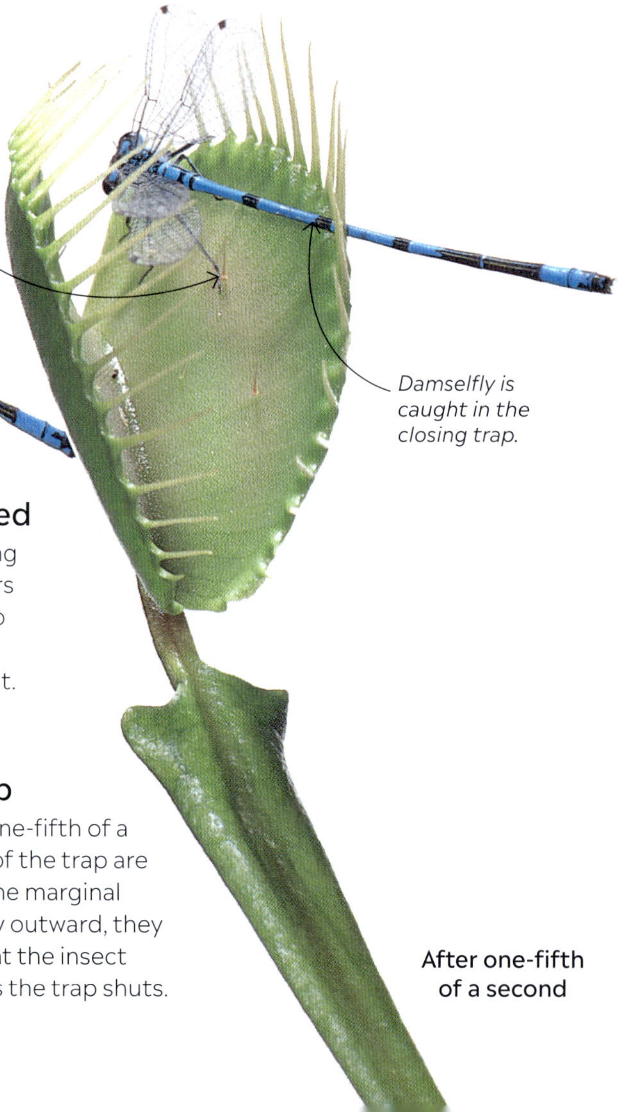

Lower part of the leaf

Open trap

After one-fifth of a second

42

Novelty plant

The first living specimen of the Venus flytrap arrived in England from America in the mid-18th century. It aroused great curiosity among botanists. Today, Venus flytraps can be grown in pots, but indoor plants rarely flower.

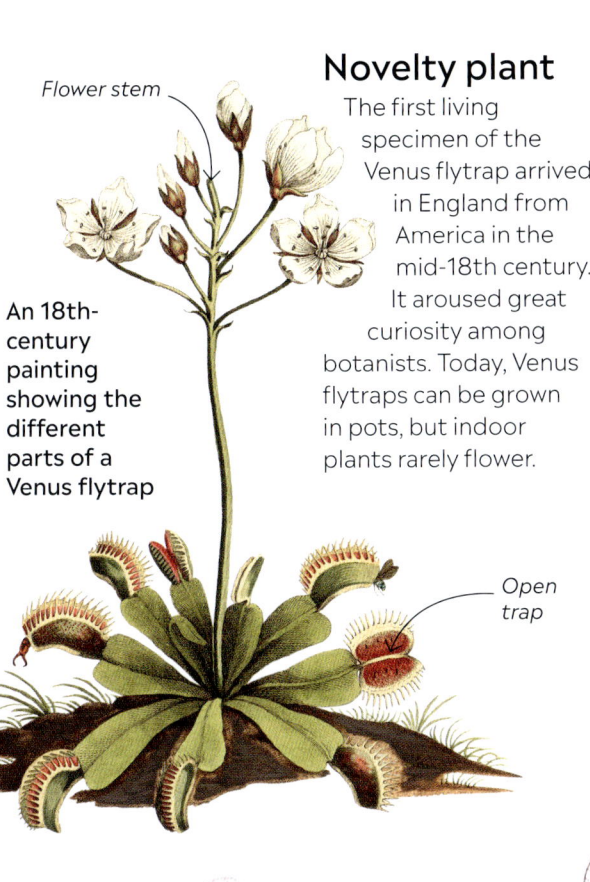

Flower stem

An 18th-century painting showing the different parts of a Venus flytrap

Open trap

Watery habitat

Venus flytraps come from the bogs of North Carolina in the US. They grow from small rhizomes and produce several traps. After catching about three insects, the traps wither.

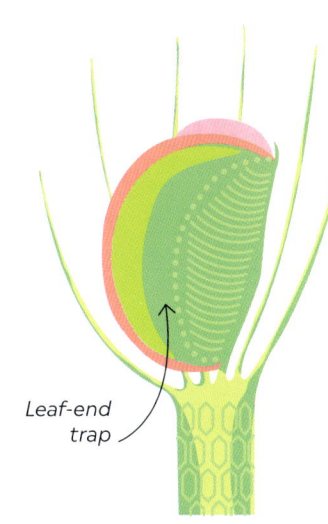

Leaf-end trap

Floating traps

This small waterwheel plant belongs to the same family as sundews and the Venus flytrap. Their traps catch tiny water animals, closing in one-fiftieth of a second.

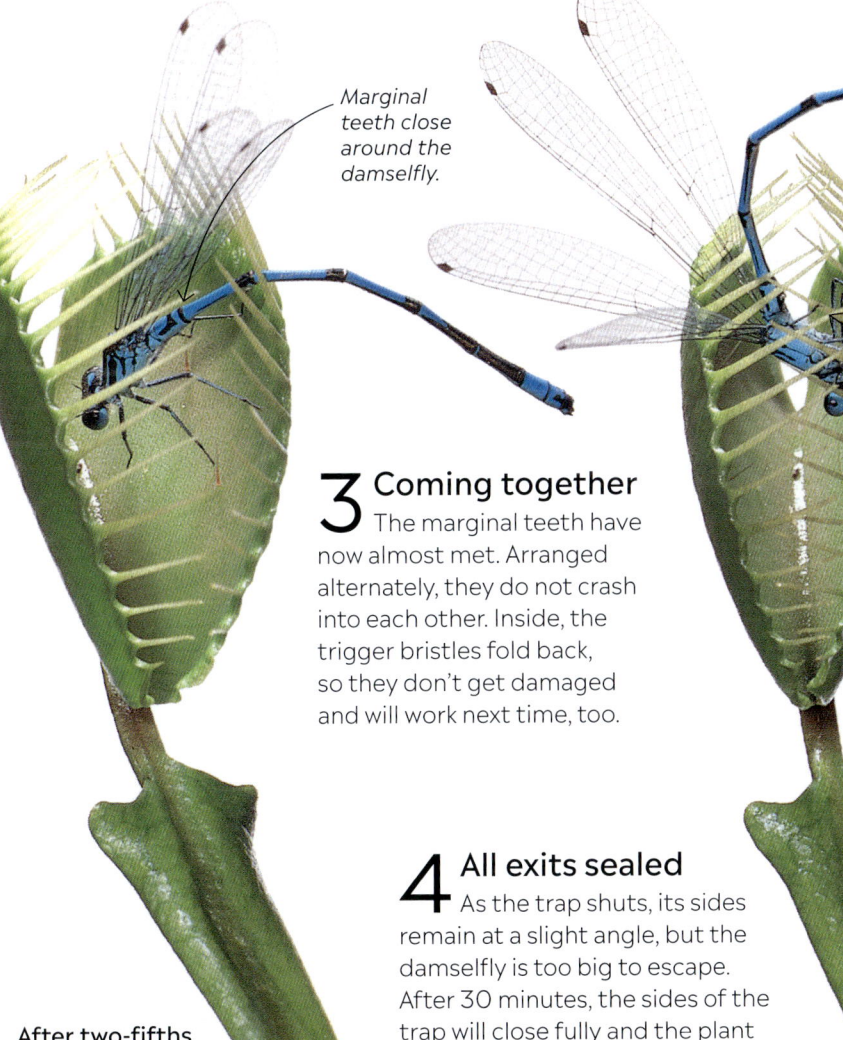

Marginal teeth close around the damselfly.

Marginal teeth form a cage around the damselfly.

3 Coming together
The marginal teeth have now almost met. Arranged alternately, they do not crash into each other. Inside, the trigger bristles fold back, so they don't get damaged and will work next time, too.

The trap is almost closed.

After two-fifths of a second

4 All exits sealed
As the trap shuts, its sides remain at a slight angle, but the damselfly is too big to escape. After 30 minutes, the sides of the trap will close fully and the plant can begin to digest its prisoner.

5 Digestion
Inside, glands secrete acid and enzymes that will slowly digest all the soft parts of the insect, which will be absorbed by the same glands. After two weeks, the trap opens, ready for a new meal.

Plant **parasites**

Parasitic plants steal the food made by their host plants, and most do not need sunlight. They attach themselves to the stems or roots of their hosts with suckers, known as haustoria. The suckers penetrate the host's food channels and absorb the sugars and minerals that the parasitic plant needs. Some, such as mistletoe, can use sunlight to make food, too.

The flowers are mostly reddish or purplish brown.

Giant rafflesia flower
Each flower weighs nearly 15 lb (7 kg), and reaches up to 3 ft (1 m) in diameter. The flower fills the air with a putrid smell that attracts pollinating flies. This plant is the largest of 50 species of rafflesia, all of them completely parasitic.

👁 EYEWITNESS

Chris Thorogood
British botanist Chris Thorogood has been fascinated by parasitic plants, particularly rafflesia, since childhood. He treks through remote rainforests in Southeast Asia to study these plants and find effective ways to save them from extinction.

Mistletoe
Mistletoe, once sacred to druids, has become part of Christmas traditions.

Thick and
fleshy sepals

Stinking giant

The rafflesia, the world's
heaviest flower, lives on
vine roots in Southeast
Asia. It has no roots,
stems, or leaves, and
appears above ground
only when it blooms.

Making a break-in

Dodder stems
spread over their
hosts like tangled
string. Young dodders
have roots, but the
roots wither as haustoria
penetrate the host's
food channels.

Dodder
flowers

*Dodder stem
twisting around
the stem of its
host plant*

Haustoria
penetrating the
stem of the host

Dodder
flowers

45

Passenger plants

Species that grow on larger plants without using them for food are known as epiphytic plants. Many can get all the water they need by absorbing it from the air or by collecting it in structures formed for the purpose. They extract minerals from trickling rainwater and plant debris. Being an epiphyte gives a small plant a chance to collect a lot of light without the need for tall stems. Most live in tropical and subtropical regions, where there is lots of moisture in the air.

Forest climbers

These large, woody climbers, known as lianas, grow in the forests of Central America.

Orchid leaves have a special coating that reduces water loss.

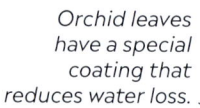

A big bromeliad can hold more than 1 gallon (5 liters) of water.

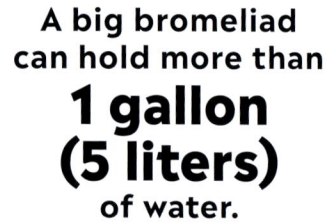

Orchids in the canopy

Private pond

Bromeliads are a family of plants that includes the pineapple. Their stiff leaves channel rainwater into a central reservoir (below). Hairs on the leaves then absorb the water so the plant can use it.

High-rise flowers

Looking for light, epiphytic orchids grow high up in the trees in the humid, tropical forests of Sri Lanka.

Central reservoir

A species of
moth orchid

Epiphytic orchids

There are up to 25,000 species of orchids. Tropical orchids that live by perching on other plants all have three types of aerial roots: some cling to the host, some absorb minerals, and some extract water from the atmosphere.

Flowers produce minute seeds to be dispersed by wind.

Thick, trailing aerial roots collect moisture and minerals from trickling rainwater.

Liana stems make a natural rope.

Natural ropes

Lianas are climbing plants with flexible woody stems. Rooted in the ground, they use trees for support, and some also twine around each other. Strangler species begin in the canopy and grow downward.

Life in **water**

The first plants on Earth evolved in water. Today, only a few flowering plants, such as eelgrasses, live in the sea—far more live in ponds, lakes, and rivers. Most of them are rooted to the bottom, but some have no roots and receive all the nutrients they need from the water instead of the soil.

Glossy yellow flowers attract pollinating insects.

Greater spearwort

Unopened bud

Historic hideout
In the Bible, a pharaoh's daughter found baby Moses among bulrushes in the Nile River.

Above water
The greater spearwort is an emergent water plant. It starts its annual cycle of growth underwater but soon reaches the surface. It grows up to 2 ft (60 cm) above the water.

Spear-shaped leaves

Leaves of the giant water lily are strong enough to support a newborn baby's weight.

Fanwort

Leaves under water
The finely divided leaves of the fanwort are not damaged by the current.

Leaves are ⅕–⅘ in (5–20 mm) long.

River giant

The floating leaves of the Amazonian water lily can reach a diameter of more than 6 ft (2 m).

Upturned edges on leaves give this plant the name "water platter."

Papyrus plants

Plant for paper

Papyrus is a giant reed, reaching up to 9 ft (3 m). In ancient Egypt, it was used to make paper to write on.

Tough, waxy surface repels water.

Flexible stalks attach the leaves to the roots, anchored in the muddy bottom.

Water lily

Flowers bloom above the surface.

Floating on the surface

When young, water lily leaves are rolled up under water like short tubes. In spring, they reach the surface and open out to form flat pads. When water lilies completely cover a pond, they prevent submerged plants from getting light.

Above the **snow line**

Plants growing at high altitudes have specific problems to overcome. Thin mountain air holds little heat, and on exposed mountainsides, strong winds roar free and increase the wind chill factor. Low rainfall and thin, frozen soil mean that water is scarce. But many plants have clever adaptations to survive the harsh conditions. In the Himalayas of Asia, flowering plants have been found at more than 20,000 ft (6,000 m), sheltering in rock cracks and hollows.

Quick work

In spring, mountain slopes burst into color. Alpine plants do not have long to flower and make seeds before the cold returns.

Hairy leaves

The leaves of mountain avens have fine hairs underneath to keep water in and the cold out.

Mountain avens

Mountain kidney vetch

Built-in sunscreen

Growing high in the Alps, mountain kidney vetch has hairy leaves for insulation and UV light protection.

Radiation hazard

The silversword, growing at high altitude in Hawaii, has fine white hairs. They protect it from the sun's ultraviolet radiation.

Plant cushions

This evergreen dwarf hebe has small tough leaves that can take frost. It grows in dense cushions that trap heat, prevent wind damage, and reduce water loss.

Dwarf hebe, New Zealand

Flat mats

Many alpine plants spread out close to the ground, keeping out of icy winds. *Mazus reptans* forms large mats in the Himalayas.

Mazus reptans

Alpine daphne

Mini shrub

The alpine daphne is a lot smaller than daphnes that grow at lower levels.

Alpine moltkias

Small leaves

Alpine moltkias have slender leaves to better withstand strong mountain winds.

Mounds of color

The bright flowers of this phlox stand out against the rocky slopes and attract pollinators.

Alpine phlox

Dual protection

Mountain rock roses stand up to strong winds better than those with taller, rigid stems. Fine hairs on leaves and stems also protect the plant.

Rock rose

Two ways to spread

This storksbill spreads both with seeds and with its creeping root system.

Mountain dwarf

Many mountain plants, such as St. John's wort, are smaller than their lowland relatives.

St. John's wort

Storksbill

Conserving water

Succulents are able to survive for years in very dry regions. They have evolved ways of collecting as much water as possible during rare downpours and store it for later use. Many succulents have very long roots, which grow near the surface, so when it rains, these plants can collect water from a wider area. Many open the pores (stomata) on their leaves only at night, when the air is cool and less water evaporates. Some, such as cacti, reduce water loss by having no leaves at all.

Barrel
cactus

Fish-hook
cactus

Many cacti have beautiful flowers.

Hedgehog
cactus

The cactus family
Almost all true cacti come from the Americas. Most cacti have very thick stems and thick groups of spines instead of normal leaves. Ridges down their stems allow them to expand to store rain water.

Cross section of square stem

Row of spines

Clusters of spines

Spurge

Similar traits
The plant on the far left is a spurge. It has adapted to its dry habitat, like the two cacti to its right—it has no leaves and its stem holds water.

Prickly pear
cactus

Cleistocactus

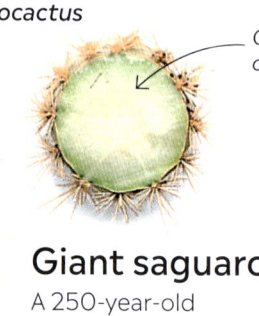

Cross section of round stem

Giant saguaro
A 250-year-old saguaro can be 65 ft (20 m) tall and weigh 6.6 tons.

Succulents

Plants with fleshy leaves or stems for storing water are known as succulents. There are three main types of succulents. Stem succulents, such as cacti, store water in their stems and tend to live in the driest climates. Leaf succulents store water in their leaves and grow in damper conditions. Root succulents hold water in their thickened roots.

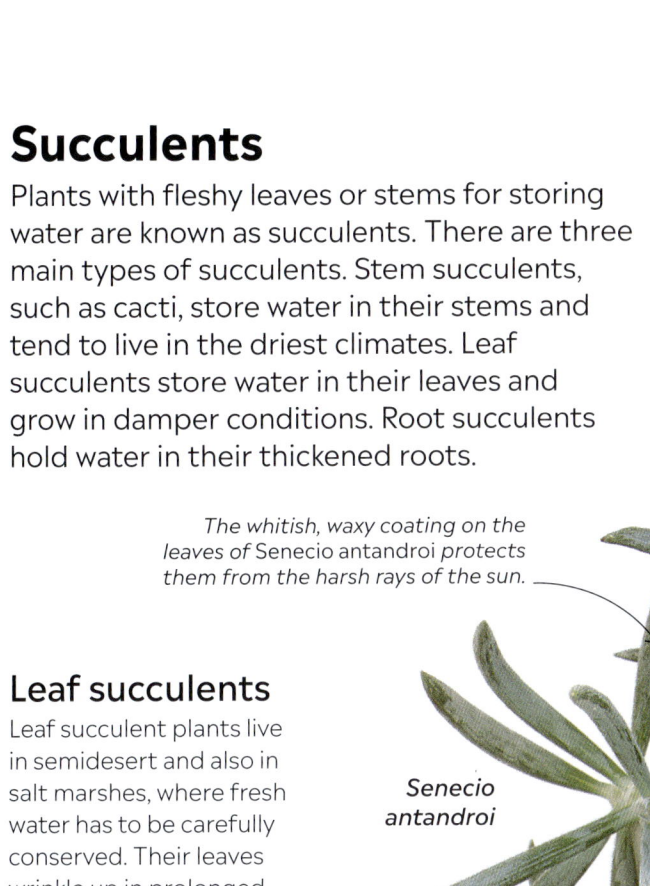

Cotyledon

Blue echeveria

The leaves of this cotyledon are fleshy and have a waxy surface to reduce water loss.

The whitish, waxy coating on the leaves of Senecio antandroi protects them from the harsh rays of the sun.

Leaf succulents

Leaf succulent plants live in semidesert and also in salt marshes, where fresh water has to be carefully conserved. Their leaves wrinkle up in prolonged dry weather, but when it rains, they swell again.

Senecio antandroi

The plump leaves of Haworthia cymbiformis are swollen with stored water.

Necklace vine leaves look as if they have been threaded on a string.

Necklace vine

Panda plant

Blue echeveria

Haworthia cymbiformis

Panda plant

Senecio antandroi

Cotyledon

Necklace vine

Drought-proof leaves

Up to nine-tenths of the weight of a succulent leaf may be water. Leaves have a waxy coating that hinders water from evaporating through the leaf surface.

Fleeting flowers

Many desert plants are ephemerals, such as these sand sunflowers in the Utah Desert. They germinate only after rain and then bloom, make seeds, and die very rapidly.

Market in Peru
Potatoes originated in the high Andes of South America. A great many varieties are still grown and sold there.

Growing foods

Plants have been cultivated as food crops for thousands of years. When the first farmers gathered seeds to produce crops for the following year, they took them from the healthiest plants. Over time, crops improved, and this process continues today. Different species were grown in different regions, but now we can eat crops from around the world.

Kept in the dark
Wild chicory has a bitter taste. To reduce bitterness, the plant is cut back to the ground to regrow in almost no light. This also turns it pale.

Modern corn cob

Primitive form of corn plant and cob

Pale shoot of cultivated chicory

Corn cultivation
Corn, or maize, is a cereal—like wheat and rice, it is a member of the grass family. It was first cultivated in Central America. Selective breeding has changed the size and shape of its cobs.

Wild chicory

👁 EYEWITNESS

Alice Waters
American chef Alice Waters promotes healthy living and sustainable agriculture. Through "The Edible Schoolyard" and "The School Lunchbox" initiatives in California, she has established school gardens. Here, students are taught how to grow and cook their own organic crops.

Small tomatoes like these first grew wild in South America.

Tomato flowers

Cultivated tomatoes

Tomato sizes
The tomato's wild ancestor was a small red berry. Today, both small and big tomatoes are cultivated.

Growing in water
Rice, first cultivated in Asia some 5,000 years ago, grows in water-filled paddy fields.

Flower head of wild carrot

Paddy field

Wild carrot root

Cultivated carrot

Edible roots
The wild carrot is found all over Europe and through much of Asia, but its roots are white or only slightly colored.

Wild cabbage has dark green, leathery leaves.

Crunchier cabbages
The wild cabbage grows near the sea. Its leathery leaves are loosely arranged on a branched stem. Modern cabbages have a less bitter taste and juicier, often crinkly leaves that are packed tightly together in a round shape.

Wild cabbage

Modern cabbage

Modern red cabbage

A wide variety
This 16th-century painting by Lucas van Valckenborch shows vegetables available in Europe at that time.

The story of wheat

Food for the masses
People have grown wheat for food for thousands of years, as this scene from the 11th century shows.

Wheat has been cultivated by humans as a valuable source of food for at least 9,000 years. It started in the region known as the Fertile Crescent, which includes part of modern-day Iraq, Iran, Israel, and Turkey, but wheat is now grown in most parts of the world. Modern varieties have higher yields, resist drought, and can withstand disease, but ancient grains are also cultivated for their taste.

Easier to harvest
Grains of cultivated wheat stay on the stalk rather than dropping on the ground.

Grains of wild einkorn

Grains of emmer

Wild einkorn
This wild grass is probably one of the ancestors of all cultivated wheats. It has long, thin stalks and small heads.

Einkorn
The small grains of this early wheat are nutritious but hard to thresh. It is used as health food and for animal feed.

Wild emmer
This wild grass is the ancestor of emmer, another primitive wheat. The heads and grains are larger than those of einkorn.

Emmer
Emmer was the chief cereal in ancient Greek and Roman times. It is one of the ancestors of modern cultivated wheat.

Spelt

A leap forward came when emmer crossed with wild goat grass, a weed growing in fields. The result was spelt wheat, which is still cultivated.

Wheatfield prairie

The world's major wheat-producing countries, such as China, India, and the US, grow wheat in vast fields. Modern wheat has been bred to have shorter stalks, making it easier to harvest than long stalks that bend over.

Spelt grains

Long, spiky bristles, or awns, attach to scales around each grain.

Spelt

Durum wheat

Pasta shells

Brown bread made of whole grain flour

Durum wheat

Another large-grain wheat closely related to emmer is durum wheat. It provides the flour for pasta and cookies. Because its gluten content is low, it does not make good bread.

Bread wheat grains

Whole grain flour

Bread wheat

Bread wheat

The most widely grown wheat is also a hybrid of emmer and wild goat grass. Its large grains have a high gluten content, good for light, airy bread.

White bread, made from finely ground, bleached flour

57

Potions and poisons

Since ancient times, certain plant species have been used as cures. The chemicals they produce may be dangerous in large quantities, but small amounts can prove very useful in the treatment of some illnesses.

Aloe vera

Jojoba

Lotion made from aloe vera

Soothing cosmetics

Jojoba and aloe vera contain oils that help keep skin soft.

Prized root

Powdered ginseng, used in east Asia for 5,000 years, has a stimulant effect.

Red ginseng root

Mixed bag

Oil from the beans of the castor-oil plant has been used as a cure of many ailments since ancient times. But the beans also contain ricin, a lethal poison.

Castor-oil plant

Beans contain oil and poisonous ricin.

Opium poppy

Raw opium is the poppy's dried sap. It is used in morphine, codeine, and heroin—drugs that can be deadly.

Opium poppies

Detail from a 12th-century herbal (book on medicinal plants)

A qreaf iquidemde cocofindos.
Q uidamficamellam cam uocit

Leopard lily plant
If swallowed, this plant's poisonous sap makes the mouth swell so much that talking becomes difficult.

Leaves of the leopard lily

Drink or drug?
The mescal cactus contains mescaline, which causes hallucinations. The drink Mezcal, however, is made from the agave plant.

Mescal cactus

Alcoholic drink

Belladonna
The drug atropine, used in eye surgery, is made from the poisonous belladonna plant.

Coca leaves

Coca leaves
Traditionally chewed in the Andes, to ease tiredness, coca leaves contain cocaine, an addictive drug.

Foxglove

Tonic water, containing quinine

Belladonna, or deadly nightshade

Help for hearts
The leaves of the foxglove contain a substance that helps the heart beat more slowly and strongly. But big doses can cause palpitations or dizziness.

A cure for malaria
Quinine, used to treat malaria, is obtained from the bark of South American cinchona trees.

Leaves from the cinchona tree, whose bark is used to make quinine

59

The plant collectors

Many of the plants that have become common in gardens all over the world are, in fact, very far from home. Tulips originally came from Central Asia, fuchsias from South America, and wisteria from China and Japan. Botanists traveled far and wide, especially in the 19th and early 20th centuries, collecting plants and seeds to grow at home.

A 19th-century plant collector with his collecting case

Scutellaria tournefortii

Plant named after Joseph Pitton de Tournefort

Royal mission

Sent out by Louis XIV, Joseph Pitton de Tournefort (1656–1708) collected plants along eastern Mediterranean shores.

Plant paradise

Asia has always been of great interest to botanists. On the left is Frank Kingdon-Ward, an English botanist who explored China, Myanmar, and India for up to 50 years, collecting seeds of many rare plants. To the right, a modern-day botanist in India is at work.

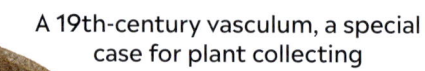

A 19th-century vasculum, a special case for plant collecting

Sarcococca hookeriana *is named after the Hookers.*

British botanists

William Hooker (1785–1865) was the first director of the Royal Botanic Gardens at Kew, England. His son, Joseph (1817–1911), collected plants in the Himalayas.

Mexianthus mexicanus

The plant is named after Ynés Mexía.

Fit for royalty

The earliest recorded botanical expedition was in 1495 BCE. Collectors brought back myrrh and frankincense trees from the Horn of Africa for Egypt's Queen Hatshepsut.

Groundbreaking work

Mexican American botanist Ynés Mexía (1870–1938) traveled alone through the Americas in the early 1900s, collecting plants. Her collection includes more than 145,000 plant specimens, with many named after her. She was also an ardent conservationist who spoke about preserving the redwood trees in California.

18th-century botanical books

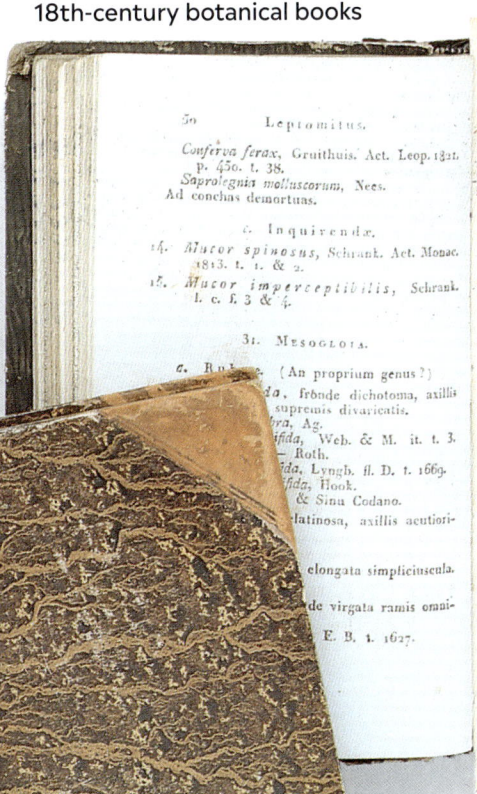

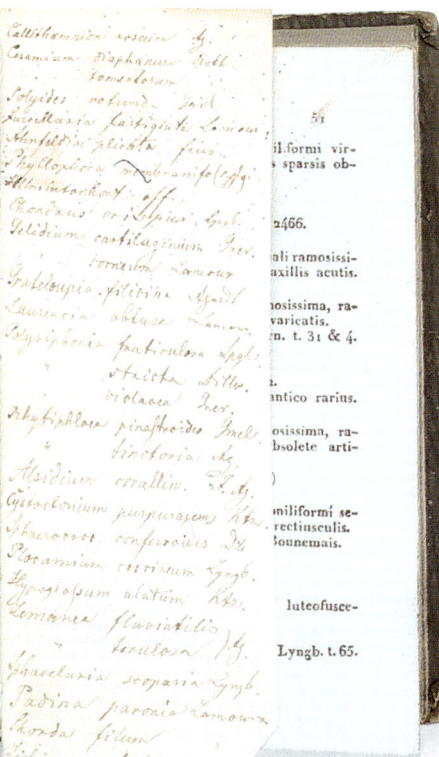

In disguise

In the 1700s, when women were banned from sailing on ships in France, explorer Jeanne Baret disguised herself as a man and collected more than 6,000 plant species during her voyage.

Looking at **plants**

There are two types of plant collections. A herbarium consists of preserved specimens, usually pressed. Collections of living plants are equally important and sometimes ensure that rare plant species do not die out. Making your own collection of flowers and pressing them is a good way to learn about plants, but make sure not to uproot wild flowers.

Herbarium specimen sheet

Preserving bottle for fleshy plant parts such as flowers and fruits

Box with a dried specimen

HERB. HORT. REG. B

Na echinacea

Forest, Lincs

HERB. HORT. BOT. REG. KEW.

47817

Dendrobium (lindleyi) aggregatum Rol

Thailand

Menzies & Poh
89

Plant press

Botanist treasure

A herbarium contains pressed specimens mounted on a sheet, with labels saying where and when they were found. This can be used by botanists to study plants in detail.

Pruning shears for cutting hardy material

Trowel for digging up roots

Learning more

Drawing or photographing flowers is a great way of studying them. Magnifying glasses are useful for examining leaves and petals. Collecting seeds and growing plants from them requires patience and care. Many seeds will germinate better if they are left in a fridge for a few weeks before planting.

Sketch pad

Magnifying glass

Scissors

Camera

Envelopes for collecting seeds

Drying flowers

In a screw press, specimens are laid between sheets of absorbent paper, which should be changed, until the plant is dry.

Base of screw press

Absorbent paper

Simple screw press

Screws for tightening the press

Top of screw press

63

Did you know?

AMAZING FACTS

Bristlecone pine tree

• The oldest individual living plant is thought to be a bristlecone pine (*Pinus longaeva*). Named Methuselah, it is nearly 4,900 years old. It lives in the White Mountains of California, US, but its exact location is kept secret to protect it from harm.

• The orchid family has more species than any other flowering plant, with 25,000–30,000 species recognized, mostly in tropical regions. Orchids are found in every continent except for Antarctica, inhabiting just about every type of environment, except for extreme deserts and salt water.

• The oldest seeds known to germinate and grow into a plant come from the date palm (*Phoenix dactylifera*) and are thought to be 2,000 years old. These seeds were found near the Dead Sea in Israel.

• The fynbos, or evergreen bushland, of the Cape region in South Africa contains one of the world's most dense concentrations of plant species within a small area. The eastern and northern coasts around Cape Town are home to an amazing range of aloes, proteas, and ericas. There are more than 8,500 plant species in this tiny region. This is almost as many as in the whole of the continent of Europe.

• Sphagnum moss, which is found in bogs and contributes to the formation of peat, can soak up more than 25 times its own dry weight in moisture.

• As plants get smaller, we know less about them. Scientists estimate that they have identified 85–90 percent of flowering plants, but only about 5 percent of the world's microscopic plant organisms.

• The largest fruit is the pumpkin, which can weigh up to 2,702 lb (1,226 kg). Its close rival is the squash, which has been known to grow to 2,164 lb (981 kg).

• The main ingredient in chocolate is the bean of the cacao tree, which first grew in the rainforests of South America. Indigenous peoples in the region began using cacao beans several thousand years ago.

• Fossils of the still-existing ginkgo tree (*Ginkgo biloba*) date back some 200 million years. It first appeared at the time of the dinosaurs, during the Jurassic period. Today, extract from the bark and root of the tree is considered to have medicinal benefits for humans. The seed kernel of the tree is a delicacy in China.

• The raffia palm (*Raphia ruffia*) of Madagascar and Africa's tropical eastern coast has the world's largest leaves, measuring up to 66 ft (20 m) in length.

• The banyan tree (*Ficus benghalensis*) has aerial roots that grow down from the tree's branches and eventually form new trunks. In this way, the banyan grows both upward and downward.

• Japan greatly values the flower of the chrysanthemum and includes its emblem on the national flag. The country has dedicated a whole day to the flower, September 9. The *feng shui* tradition teaches that the chrysanthemum brings laughter and happiness to a home.

• Tulips were originally native to Türkiye, Iran, Syria, and parts of Asia, before being brought to Europe by traveling merchants in the 16th century. The Dutch were the first European nation to cultivate tulips, in 1593. By 1633, the Dutch upper classes were so gripped by tulip mania that individual bulbs were sold for vast amounts of money.

• A plant called St. Mary's bean, from Central America, has the greatest known range for drifting seeds. Its seeds have been washed up in the Marshall Islands, in the Pacific Ocean, and also on the coast of Norway—places that are around 15,000 miles (24,150 km) apart.

Date palm

Protea

Orchid

QUESTIONS AND ANSWERS

Red cherry fruits

Why are the fruits of the cherry plant red?

The fruits of the cherry plant are bright red in color to attract birds to eat the fruits. The cherry fruits contain seeds that have a hard protective covering. This ensures that when the seeds are eaten by a bird, they pass unharmed through the bird's digestive system. In this way, the seeds are safely spread, and the plant guarantees the survival of its offspring. Plants pollinated by insects are rarely red because insects, with the exception of butterflies, cannot see the color red.

Which plant is considered to be the most bizarre of all?

Welwitschia mirabilis, also known as the tumboa, from the Namib Desert in Africa, is one of the strangest plants in the world. Known to live for up to 2,000 years, it has a stumpy stem and just two straplike leaves, which grow nonstop throughout its life. As the plant ages, its leaves become twisted and gnarled, and they eventually can be many feet long. The leaves are tough and woody—an adaptation that helps prevent them from being eaten or drying out. *Welwitschia* survives in a region where there is little rain. But fog rolls in from the sea and the plant's leaves gather moisture from the fog. *Welwitschia* does not grow flowers but produces seeds in cones.

What is the richest plant region of the world?

South America, which holds an estimated 90,000 species, is the world's richest plant region. Brazil is the country with the greatest known number of plant species, at 56,000, followed by Colombia, with 35,000 species. Mexico, Venezuela, Ecuador, Bolivia, and Peru are not far behind. The proliferation of plant species in this part of the world is thought to be due to the moist habitat associated with its tropical rainforests.

Why do some tree leaves change color in fall?

As the days become colder and shorter, chlorophyll, the green pigment in the leaves, flows back into the tree. Meanwhile, waste products, such as tannins, pass out into the leaves. This chemical change produces browns and reds in the leaves as they die. Trees that lose their leaves are said to be deciduous.

RECORD BREAKERS

Smallest plant
The world's smallest flowering plant is watermeal (*Wolffia australiana*). A tablespoon can hold more than 100,000 plants, with each measuring only 1/50 in (0.6 mm) long and 1/100 in (0.3 mm) wide.

Watermeal

Largest seed
The largest seed produced by any plant is that of the coco-de-mer (*Lodoicea maldivica*), from the Seychelles. This palm, also known as the double coconut tree, produces seeds that weigh up to 55 lb (25 kg) and take up to 10 years to grow into a tree.

Tallest tree
The redwood tree called Hyperion (*Sequoia sempervirens*), found in California, is the world's tallest tree, reaching a maximum height of 380 ft (115 m).

Welwitschia mirabilis

Ginkgo, also called maidenhair

Classification

The plant kingdom contains about 400,000 known species, divided into different groups. Most plants belong to the flowering plant family, or angiosperms. Plants that have seeds but no flowers are called gymnosperms.

Liverwort

Ginkgo

The ginkgo, native to China, is a gymnosperm. It is related to conifers but forms a group of its own. It is deciduous and has fan-shaped leaves.

Mosses and liverworts

Mosses and liverworts belong to a group called the bryophytes, which number 14,000 species. These small plants usually grow in shaded, damp places.

FLOWERING PLANTS

Wheat

Flowering plants, or angiosperms, constitute about 250,000 known species. Flowers are specialized parts of plants. They must be pollinated so that seeds develop and then get dispersed, to ensure the continuation of each species. There are two types of flowering plants—monocots and dicots.

Rose

Monocots have a single cotyledon, or seed leaf. Their adult leaves are often long and narrow, with parallel veins. Monocots include orchids and lilies; cereals, such as wheat; some vegetables, such as leeks; and some fruits, such as pineapples.

Dicots have two cotyledons, or seed leaves. Adult leaves usually have a network of veins around a central midrib. There are at least 200,000 species, also including all broadleaved trees.

Dicot plants often have woody stems.

Pineapple

Leek

Cabbage

Cactus

Ferns

The pteridophytes, or ferns, include around 12,000 species. Their leaves, known as fronds, carry spores, which produce tiny plants that reproduce in turn, giving rise to new ferns.

Club mosses

Club mosses, or lycophytes, existed 430 million years ago. Today, club mosses are small, with creeping stems and overlapping leaves. They reproduce by growing spores.

Club moss

Conifers

These gymnosperms are large evergreen trees that can photosynthesize in winter and often have needle-shaped leaves. Around 550 species include firs, spruces, pines, and cedars.

Pine

Cycads

There are around 100 species of cycads, gymnosperms that grow in tropical regions. Despite being similar in appearance to palms, they are not related to them.

Cycad

Horsetails

These ancient plants are also called sphenophytes. Some 300 million years ago, they could grow 49 ft (15 m) tall. Today's species reach around 3 ft (1 m).

Horsetail

Cones are produced during the summer months.

Gnetophytes

Although they are gymnosperms, these cone-bearing desert plants resemble flowering plants in many ways. There are about 70 species.

Welwitschia mirabilis, also known as the tumboa

Find out more

Explore your own garden if you have one, or start growing a window box. Get a plant identification handbook and go for a walk in your local park or countryside. For more exotic species and a wealth of information, visit a botanical garden, or to check out ancient plant fossils, take a trip to a natural history museum.

If an area of land is privately owned, always seek permission to visit from the owner.

Botanical gardens

A botanical garden has plants from around the world. Rare and exotic species are cultivated, often in controlled environments, such as greenhouses.

Go wild

To look at plants in their natural setting, head for your local countryside (after informing an adult). Spring is a good time to see new shoots and budding flowers.

Wild flowers should not be plucked, as this disturbs the natural environment.

This garden pansy will lose some of its color as it dries.

Write the name of the plant and the date it was picked on the sheet of paper.

Drying flowers

Place a flower head and leaves flat on a sheet of blotting paper. Fold and place the sheet inside a heavy book and let dry.

Ornamental bunches

Preserve a bouquet by taking it out of water. When the stems have dried out, tie them with a ribbon.

Bunch of dried flowers

Garden growth

If you have access to a garden, use a notebook to log the development of various plant species through the seasons.

Woodland walks

Many officially organized countryside walks choose routes suited to a specific time of year. The image below shows people following a path through springtime bluebells.

Room with a view

Window boxes make great miniature gardens. Flowers and herbs can be grown in any container and placed on a window ledge or balcony.

The soil should be loose and moist before seeds are planted.

Glossary

ACHENE   A dry, one-seeded fruit. All plants in the buttercup family have achenes.

ALGA   A simple nonflowering plant that usually lives in water. Algae include seaweeds and many microscopic species.

ANGIOSPERM   A flowering plant. Angiosperms grow their seeds inside a protective case called an ovary, which develops to form a fruit.

ANNUAL   A plant that completes its life cycle within the growing season of one year.

ANTHER   The tip of a flower's stamen containing pollen.

AXIL   The angle between the upper part of a stem and a leaf or branch, where buds develop.

AXIS   The main stem or root.

BIENNIAL   A plant that has two growing seasons before it dies. The seed is sown in the first year, and flowers and fruits in its second year.

BOTANY   The scientific study of plants.

BRACT   A small, leaflike flap that grows just beneath a flower.

BUD   The first visible sign of a new limb of a plant, or the protective case that encloses a flower that is still growing inside.

BULB   An underground stem that stores food inside layers of fleshy scales. Most plants use bulbs to survive drought or cold.

BULBIL   A small bud that grows into an independent plant.

BURR   The prickly seed case of some plants.

CALYX   The ring of sepals that protects a flower bud. The calyx often falls off when the flower blooms.

Green alga, or seaweed

Bulb

Daffodil bulbs

CARPEL   The female organ of a flower, holding the stigma, the style, and the ovary.

CELL   The smallest possible unit of living matter, visible only under a microscope. A cell consists of a nucleus surrounded by a fluid called cytoplasm, inside a cell wall.

CHLOROPHYLL   The green pigment present in all plants and algae and involved in the process of photosynthesis.

CHLOROPLAST   A microscopic green structure that contains chlorophyll. Found inside plant cells, chloroplasts capture energy from the sunlight.

CLIMBER   A plant that grows upward and outward, attaching itself to structures such as walls and fences.

COROLLA   The ring of petals in a flower.

COTYLEDON   A specialized leaf that is prepacked inside a seed. Cotyledons can look quite different from ordinary leaves.

DECIDUOUS   A plant that loses its leaves every fall.

DICOT   A plant whose seeds have two cotyledons (seed leaves). The leaves of a dicot, or dicotyledon, are often broad, and they have veins arranged in a network.

EMBRYO   A young plant in its earliest stages of development.

ENDOSPERM   A supply of food that is stored inside a seed. The endosperm fuels the seedling's early growth.

EVERGREEN   A plant that retains its leaves all year round, such as pines and firs.

FILAMENT   The stalk of a stamen, which supports the anther.

FLORET   A small flower that forms part of a composite flower, or flower head.

GERMINATION   When a seed begins to sprout and grow.

GYMNOSPERM   A plant whose seeds do not develop inside an ovary. Most gymnosperms are coniferous trees.

HARDY   Being able to withstand extremes of temperature, such as cold and frost.

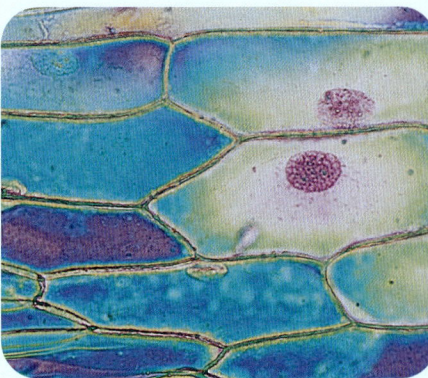

Microscopic view of typical plant cells

MONOCOT   A plant whose seeds have a single cotyledon (seed leaf). The leaves of a monocot, or monocotyledon, usually have parallel veins.

NECTAR   A naturally occurring sweet liquid found in the glands of many flowers.

OVARY   A female reproductive organ, which encloses fertilized seeds.

OVULE   A collection of female cells that form a seed after they have been fertilized by pollen.

PAPPUS   A ring or parachute of very fine hair that grows above a seed and helps it to be dispersed by the wind.

PARASITE   An organism that lives in or on another organism, or host, from which it takes food and energy without giving anything back in return.

PERENNIAL   A plant that lasts or flowers for more than two years.

PETAL   A leafy flap in a flower, often brightly colored to attract pollinators.

Strawberry, a dicot plant

PHLOEM A system of cells that carries nutrients throughout a plant.

PHOTOSYNTHESIS The process by which plants generate their own food, occurring when a green pigment called chlorophyll reacts with sunlight, carbon dioxide, and water to make carbohydrates (glucose), water, and oxygen.

PIGMENT A colored chemical found in flowers, leaves, and stems. One pigment, chlorophyll, makes plants look green.

PLANTLET A young plant, which is sometimes attached to its parent.

PLUMULE The embryo shoot in a seed.

POLLEN Microscopic grains containing male sex cells. Pollen is produced by the anthers of flowers.

POLLINATION The process by which pollen is carried from one flower to another. The male pollen fertilizes the female ovule and creates a seed. Insects and animals carry pollen between flowering plants, or it can be blown by the wind.

RECEPTACLE The part of a plant that contains the flower, or in flowerless plants, the reproductive organs or spores.

RHIZOME A creeping underground stem. Rhizomes often sprout leaves as they push their way through the ground.

ROOT The part of a plant that anchors it to a solid surface, such as soil, and absorbs water and nutrients.

RUNNER A stem that produces new plants by growing across the ground and sprouting roots.

Poppy seeds scattered by the wind

SEED A tough structure used by plants to reproduce. A seed contains a young plant, or embryo, together with all the food reserves it needs to start growing.

SEPAL A leafy flap that protects a flower while it is still a bud. Sepals often fall off when the flower opens.

SHOOT Parts of a plant above ground, including its stems, leaves, and flowers.

SPADIX A fleshy spike of flowers.

SPATHE A leaflike hood that partly encloses a flower head.

SPECIES A group of plants, or other living things, that look similar, and that normally breed together in the wild.

SPORE A single-celled reproductive unit of some organisms.

SPUR A flowering or fruit-bearing branch that shoots out from an existing plant.

STAMEN A flower's pollen-producing part, consisting of a filament and an anther.

STARCH The main food type stored in a plant. Chemically known as a carbohydrate, this food contains vital energy reserves.

STEM The part of a plant that carries the leaves. Also known as a stalk, the stem transports water and food from the roots to the rest of the plant.

STIGMA The structure in a flower that receives pollen during pollination.

STOMA An opening through which gases enter and leave the green part of a plant.

STYLE The stalklike structure in a flower that connects the stigma with the ovary.

TAPROOT A main root growing down.

TENDRIL A threadlike part of a plant that grows outward and wraps around nearby objects, helping the plant stay upright.

TEPAL A flap around a flower that functions as both sepal and petal.

TESTA A seed's hard shell or coating.

Variegated ivy leaf

THRESH Separating seeds or grains from the crop plants mechanically.

TRANSPIRATION The movement of water through a plant. Water is taken up by the roots, and it evaporates through pores in the leaves.

TUBER A swelling or lump that forms in a root or stem and usually contains valuable food reserves for the rest of the plant. A potato is a tuber.

VARIEGATED Streaked or mottled, with contrasting colors. In plants, variegated leaves are caused by differences in the pigments across the leaf.

VEGETATION The plants found in a particular habitat, or environment.

WHORL A collection of leaves, sepals, or petals growing in a circle around a stem.

XYLEM A system of cells that carries water through a plant.

Bamboo, a monocot plant

Index

Acknowledgments

The publisher would like to thank the following for their help with making the book:
Arthur Chater, Colin Ziegler, and Trudy Brannan at the Natural History Museum; Dave King for special photography pp.8–9, and Peter Radcliffe p.63; Fred Ford and Mike Pilley at Radius for artwork; Peter Radcliffe and Steve Setford for the wallchart; Vandana Likhmania and Anna Streiffert Limerick for editorial assistance; Priya Singh and Samrajkumar S. for image administration support; Hazel Beynon for proofreading; and Elizabeth Wise for the index.

The publisher would like to thank the following for their kind permission to reproduce their images:
(Key: a-above; b-below/bottom; c-center; f-far; l-left; r-right; t-top)

Heather Angel/Biofotos: 49cl. **A.N.T./NHPA:** 25cr. **Alamy Stock Photo:** Art Directors & TRIP / Helene Rogers / ArkReligion.com 48cra, Associated Press / Paul Sakuma 54br, Krys Bailey 64bc, Pat Bennett 27cra, Sabena Jane Blackbird 46cb, Blickwinkel 50c, Ed Buziak 44br, Nigel Cattlin 39cla, Chronicle 43tl, CPA Media Pte Ltd / Pictures From History 61tr, Dembinsky Photo Associates / Carol Dembinsky

43tc, Flowerphotos 64bl, Mike Ford 39r, Brian Hird (Wildflowers) 29bl, imageBROKER.com GmbH & Co. KG / Moritz Wolf 7tl, Naki 69cr, Walter Oleksy 61c, Max Oltra 59c, Malcolm Park 8br, Pictorial Press Ltd 61br, John Plant 44–45c, Tony Roberts 10cra, Science History Images 22tr, Universal Images Group North America LLC / DeAgostini / DEA / C. DANI-I. JESKE 50bl, Wildlife Gmbh 47bc, World History Archive 49tr, Xinhua 68–69bc. **AMKK:** © Shunsuke Shiinoki / AMKK / Azuma Makoto 12ca. **J. and M. Bain/NHPA:** 11bl. **G.I. Bernard/NHPA:** 15tr, 18cr, 36c, 40cr. **Bridgeman Images:** 55cb, 58crb, Alain Gassmann 28br. **Courtesy of Smithsonian. ©2023 Smithsonian:** Robinson, B. L. 1928. Contr. Gray Herb. 80 5. 61tl. **James H. Carmichael/NHPA:** 53br. **Gene Cox/Science Photo Library:** 7c. **Stephen Dalton/NHPA:** 19tr, 22cl, 30cr, 36tr, 40cl. **P. Dayanandan/Science Photo Library:** 9tl. **Depositphotos Inc:** Araleboy 47tr. **Dreamstime. com:** Cristianzamfir 46tc, Kkistl01 32br, Konstik 48–49c, Andrew Linscott 58c, Pilar Martín 54tl, Sergey Peterman 63cl, Rabor74 65b, Tigatelu 14tl. **Gretchen A Ertl:** Rohit Karnik 9br. **Patrick Fagot/ NHPA:** 71bl. **Getty Images:** Hulton Archive / Tom Stoddart 60cr, Royal Geographical Society 60c. **Getty Images/iStock:** E+ / Pchoui 52br. **Brian**

Hawkes/NHPA: 23tl. **Jean and Fred Hort:** 24tl. **inaturalist.org:** iNaturalist NZ / Peter de Lange 7tc, 65cra. **Istituto Italiano di Tecnologia:** Emanuela Del Dottore 39tc. **E.A. Janes/NHPA:** 28crb. **Patrick Lynch/Science Photo Library:** 6c. **Mansell Collection:** 8bl, 59bc. **Mary Evans Picture Library:** 46bl, 56tl, tr, 60tr. **Science Photo Library:** Science Source / Francesco Tomasinelli 67b. **John Shaw/NHPA:** 9tr, 64tl, br. **Shutterstock.com:** Todor Stoyanov-Raveo 57tr. **Silvestris Fotoservice/FLPA:** 65tl. **Studio Petals:** Neera Joshi Pradhan 17cra. **Dr Chris Thorogood:** 44bc. **Vaysgant Visuals:** Yuri / Julie Moore 42cra. **M.I. Walker/NHPA:** 70tr. **John Walsh/Science Photo Library:** 15tl. **J. Watkins/Frank Lane Picture Agency:** 50cl. **Adam D Williams:** 58br. **Alan Williams:** 68tr. **Rogers Wilmshurst/Frank Lane:** 26tr. **David Woodfall/NHPA:** 68c. **Steven Wooster:** 69tr. **www.sproutworld.com:** Michael Stausholm 11ca.

Cover images: Front: **Dreamstime.com:** Daniel Prudek cr; Back: **Dreamstime.com:** Kira Kaplinski / Kkaplin cr, Oleksii Kriachko cra

DK WHAT WILL YOU EYEWITNESS NEXT?

 EYEWITNESS THE AMAZON

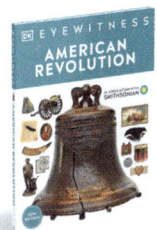 EYEWITNESS AMERICAN REVOLUTION

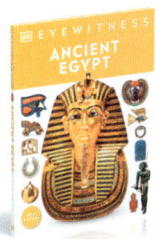 EYEWITNESS ANCIENT EGYPT

 EYEWITNESS ANCIENT GREECE

 EYEWITNESS ANCIENT ROME

 EYEWITNESS ANIMAL

 EYEWITNESS ARCTIC & ANTARCTIC

 EYEWITNESS BIRD

 EYEWITNESS CAT

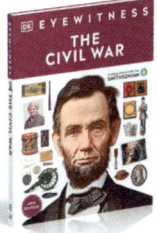 EYEWITNESS THE CIVIL WAR

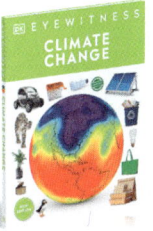 EYEWITNESS CLIMATE CHANGE

 EYEWITNESS CRYSTAL & GEM

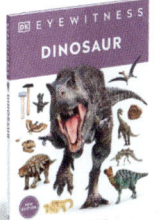 EYEWITNESS DINOSAUR

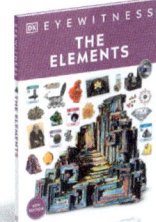 EYEWITNESS THE ELEMENTS

 EYEWITNESS FISH

 EYEWITNESS FLIGHT

 EYEWITNESS FOSSIL

 EYEWITNESS HORSE

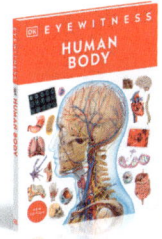 EYEWITNESS HUMAN BODY

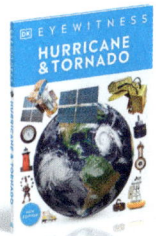 EYEWITNESS HURRICANE & TORNADO

 EYEWITNESS INSECT

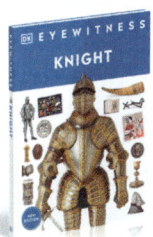 EYEWITNESS KNIGHT

 EYEWITNESS NATIONAL PARKS

 EYEWITNESS NATURAL DISASTERS

 EYEWITNESS OCEAN

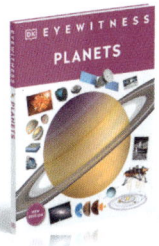 EYEWITNESS PLANETS

 EYEWITNESS PLANT

 EYEWITNESS PRESIDENTS

 EYEWITNESS REPTILE

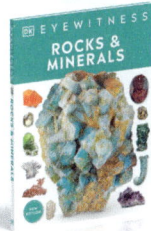 EYEWITNESS ROCKS & MINERALS

 EYEWITNESS SHARK

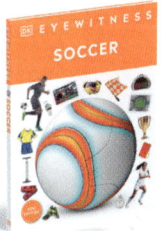 EYEWITNESS SOCCER

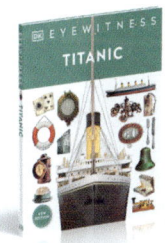 EYEWITNESS TITANIC

 EYEWITNESS TRAIN

 EYEWITNESS UNIVERSE

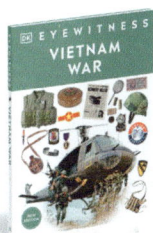 EYEWITNESS VIETNAM WAR

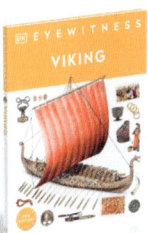 EYEWITNESS VIKING

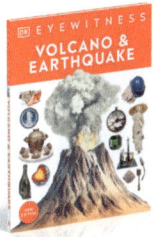 EYEWITNESS VOLCANO & EARTHQUAKE

 EYEWITNESS WEATHER

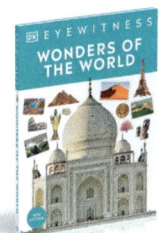 EYEWITNESS WONDERS OF THE WORLD

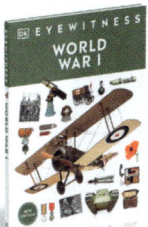 EYEWITNESS WORLD WAR I

 EYEWITNESS WORLD WAR II

Also available:

Eyewitness Amphibian
Eyewitness Ancient China
Eyewitness Ancient Civilizations
Eyewitness Arms and Armor
Eyewitness Astronomy
Eyewitness Aztec, Inca & Maya
Eyewitness Baseball
Eyewitness Bible Lands
Eyewitness Car

Eyewitness Castle
Eyewitness Chemistry
Eyewitness Dance
Eyewitness Earth
Eyewitness Eagle and Birds of Prey
Eyewitness Electricity
Eyewitness Endangered Animals
Eyewitness Forensic Science
Eyewitness Gandhi
Eyewitness Great Scientists

Eyewitness Islam
Eyewitness Judaism
Eyewitness Jungle
Eyewitness Medieval Life
Eyewitness Mesopotamia
Eyewitness Money
Eyewitness Mummy
Eyewitness Mythology
Eyewitness North American Indian
Eyewitness Pirate

Eyewitness Prehistoric Life
Eyewitness Robot
Eyewitness Science
Eyewitness Shakespeare
Eyewitness Skeleton
Eyewitness Soldier
Eyewitness Space Exploration